© 2011 MarriageKeepers Ministries, Inc. All rights reserved.

No part of this book may be reproduced, stored in a retrieval system, or transmitted by any means without written permission from the author.

First published by AuthorHouse 12/31/2010

978-0-9833205-0-0 (soft cover)
978-0-9833205-1-7 (hard cover)
978-0-9833205-2-4 (eBook)

Library of Congress Control Number: 2010917848

Printed in the United States of America

Stock images from Thinkstockphoto.com and iStockphoto.com

Because of the dynamic nature of the Internet, any Web addresses or links contained in this book may have changed since publication and may no longer be valid. The views expressed in this work are solely those of the author and do not reflect the views of the publisher, and the publisher hereby disclaims any responsibility for them.

Rob Thorpe

"husband"
A USERS GUIDE

"The principles of marriage and life are easy to understand, because Rob has clearly defined the bottom line!"

~ *Joe White, president of Kanakuk Kamps*

Foreword

*The effects of the decline of marriage on society are striking.
The failure of parents to marry and stay married
leads to more crime, poverty, mental health
problems, welfare dependency, failed schools,
blighted neighborhoods, bloated prisons, and higher rates
of single parenting and divorce in the next generation.
Nearly every major social problem has deep roots in the failure
of adults to form and sustain healthy marriages.*

~Bill Doherty, Philanthropy Roundtable, 2006

Why write another book on marriage?

I am writing primarily because knowledge from books has yet to make a significant and lasting impact on marriages and on our society. This book, by itself, won't either. But it will point husbands back to the source of "real" change—Jesus. We don't have a marriage crisis in our society; we have a Jesus crisis.

We have lost sight of the One who created marriage and who has all the knowledge and power available to allow us to enjoy this sacred relationship as it was originally intended. No amount of earthly wisdom or well-intended marriage principles will change us at our selfish core. Only the anointing and power of God's word is able to change hearts and restore broken and miserable relationships. He is enough.

My prayer is that his word will speak deeply to your masculine soul and his personal message will come through these pages to rekindle your "first love" and draw you closer to him. Marriage was created by him and for him. Only he has the ability to love through us and make us the husbands we were created to be.

Follow him, and he will make you a fabulous "husband."

~ Rob

Contents

Part One

- In the Beginning 7
- The Heart of God—for Man 9
- The Heart of God—for "Husband" 13
- What Went Wrong? 19
- The Heart of God—for You 24

Part Two

- What Do I Do with This? 28
- God's Word Specifically to Husbands 30

Part Three

- God's Word–About Relationships 48
- "We Need to Talk" 52
- Words Matter 55
- No Way, Jose' 60

Part Four

- How Do I Get There From Here? Part 1 66
- How Do I Get There From Here? Part 2 74
- Welcome To The Front Lines 79

In Closing 87

The 30-Day Challenge 90

Leaders Guide 93

Introduction

We rarely have sex anymore, and when we do, I feel like she is just "performing her wifely duty" and not out of a sense of passion or desire like it used to be. The intimacy in our marriage seems gone.

My husband doesn't seem to have any time for me anymore—or for the kids. He is always working, and when he is home, he is too tired to talk with me or to help me around the house. Somehow he finds time to go play golf or hunt with his buddies, because he says he needs to "recharge his batteries." We seem to be living in the same house but living two separate lives.

Research indicates that nearly as many Christian marriages end in divorce as marriages where the couple professes no particular religious belief. Other studies tell us that as many as 65 percent of couples feel "stuck" in an empty and unfulfilling relationship. Sadly, there are too many Christians today who simply "grin and bear" a miserable relationship and have settled for an unfulfilling marriage.

This is so far from what God intended for us in our marriage.

This book, and any other book about marriage, will not by itself help you restore a hurting marriage or magically infuse you with power and wisdom to make everything better . What this book will do is point you back to the Author of marriage and help you work on rebuilding your relationship with the only One who can fully restore the wonder, joy, and intimacy that married couples are created to experience. In doing so, you will discover his will for you as a husband and rediscover his heart for your marriage adventure.

> **We are created to know God—personally. Let's not settle to simply know "about" him. As we get to know him, he will reveal his heart for us and for our marriages. I keep asking that the God of our Lord Jesus Christ, the glorious Father, may give you the Spirit of wisdom and revelation, so that you may know him better.**
> **~ Ephesians 1:17**

> *You search the Scriptures because you think that in them you have eternal life; it is these that testify about Me; and you are unwilling to come to Me so that you may have life.* ~ John 5:39-40

Part 1

In The Beginning

Did marriage as an institution just happen, or was it deliberately designed by a loving and wise architect?

It is the foundational premise of this book that marriage is purposely designed by a Creator, Father, God. In order to more fully understand marriage and our role as husbands, it makes good sense to go back and study the original blueprint. The way to do this is to ask the Designer what he intended when he created the whole thing.

According to the Bible, God is the mastermind behind the entire concept of marriage. The book of Genesis tells us:

Then God said, "Let Us make man in Our image, according to Our likeness. They will rule the fish of the sea, the birds of the sky, the animals, all the earth, and the creatures that crawl on the earth." So God created man in His own image; He created him in the image of God; He created them male and female.
Genesis 1:26, 27

The man gave names to all the livestock, to the birds of the sky, and to every wild animal; but for the man no helper was found who was like him. So the Lord God caused a deep sleep to come over the man, and he slept. God took one of his ribs and closed the flesh at that place. Then the Lord God made the rib He had taken from the man into a woman and brought her to the man. And the man said: This one, at last, is bone of my bone, and flesh of my flesh; this one will be called woman, for she was taken from man. This is why a man leaves his father and mother and bonds with his *wife*, and they become one flesh. *Genesis 2:20 –24*

After creating man, and subsequently woman, God brought her to the man, Adam, and the first marriage took place. It is obvious that the Divine Creator of man and woman deliberately brought them together. He had a reason, a plan, and a masterful design for doing such a thing.

Let's explore …

- Why are man and woman different from the other created animals on earth?

- What was in the heart of God as he personally formed and brought them together?

- What is his divine purpose for marriage?

- How can we enjoy marriage as he intended?

- What uniquely significant role is designed for us as husbands?

The Heart of God—for Man

God created the heavens and the earth. He created all life—animal and human. But there were significant differences in how and why he created man.

1. Unlike anything else he created, God made man in his own image and blessed him.

> God said, "Let Us [Father, Son, and Holy Spirit] make mankind in Our image, after Our likeness, and let them have complete authority over the fish of the sea, the birds of the air, the beasts, and over all of the earth, and over everything that creeps upon the earth." So God created man in His own image, in the image and likeness of God He created and female He created them. And God blessed them and said to them …
> *Genesis 1:26-28*

That is a profound and awesome truth that we need to understand: *God created the first man and woman in his own image!* Think of it—God made man to be like him. Your life matters. You are significant. Truly, man is the most important being among all the creatures that God made. Only man was created in the image of God. The next time you look at your wife and are tempted to think she may be an alien from a distant galaxy, remember that she is made in God's image too—and specifically for you to help God in the process of shaping you into his man.

Also, unlike any other being that God created, man is a triune being, because he is created in the image of the triune God. "God said, 'Let us make man in Our image'" (Genesis 1:26). Man has a spiritual nature that is separate and distinct from the body in which it dwells.

The two following passages from the Bible clearly establish the fact that man is a triune being composed of spirit, soul, and body:

> I pray God your whole *spirit* and *soul* and *body* be preserved blameless unto the coming of our Lord Jesus Christ.
> 1 Thessalonians 5:23

> For the word of God is quick, and powerful, and sharper than any two-edged sword, piercing even to the dividing asunder of *soul* and *spirit*, and of the joints and marrow (body), and is a discerner of the thoughts and intents of the heart.
> Hebrews 4:12

2. Unlike anything else he created, God breathed his life into man.

> … the Lord God formed the man from the dust of the ground and breathed into his nostrils the breath of life, and the man became a living being. *Genesis 2: 7–8*

Although we are not told exactly *how* God "formed the man from dust of the ground," we know from the Creation account that God had previously created life by speaking. However, when God created man, he "breathed into his nostrils the breath of life" thereby making the man a "living creature." This speaks volumes about the heart of God toward man. No other creation received God's personal, intimate, life-giving breath. God takes dust and earth and forms a man; as if that was not astounding enough, God then breathes into his nostrils. God uses his mouth to exhale his breath of life into man. What a glorious picture! The same mouth that spoke everything into existence is now breathing man into existence.

> *Without God speaking, nothing would be. And likewise, without God breathing, man would not be. ~ Einstein*

All creation received its life and being from God. Without it, all mankind and animal kind would just be skin, organs, and bones, like a glove without a hand inside. All creation has life, and that life came from God. Man, however, was personally "crafted" by God and received life directly and personally from God's mouth.

As a triune being, man is unique in that he has a spirit. All creation has life (soul), but only man is spoken of as having a spirit. It is our spirit that can be "reborn" and through which we have the privilege of communing with our creator God.

> The lamp of the Lord searches the spirit of a man; it searches out his inmost being. *Proverbs 20:27*
>
> Jesus said: "God is a spirit; and they that worship Him must worship Him in spirit and in truth." (John 4:24)
> For who among men knows the thoughts of a man except the man's spirit within him? In the same way no one knows the thoughts of God except the Spirit of God. *1 Corinthians 2:11*
>
> The man without the Spirit does not accept the things that come from the Spirit of God, for they are foolishness to him, and he cannot understand them, because they are spiritually discerned. *1 Corinthians 2:14*

We are here on earth *for God*. We are not here for ourselves (to accumulate wealth and things, to live for pleasure, etc.) or for anything or anyone else. God created us for himself—for his pleasure and glory. God created us with the capacity to know him, commune with him, love him, and glorify him forever! The eternal God gave each of us an eternal spirit. It is God's will that we experience a deeply personal relationship with him today, tomorrow, and throughout eternity. It is for this reason that God created man in his own image.

It is our deepest need as human beings, to learn to live intimately with God. It is what we were made for
~ John Eldredge, Walking with God

3. Unlike anything else he created, God walked with and communed with man.

> And they heard the sound of the Lord God walking in the garden in the cool of the day, and Adam and his wife hid themselves from the presence of the Lord God among the trees of the garden. But the Lord God called to Adam and said to him, "Where are you?" *Genesis 3:8-9*

Adam and Eve enjoyed life as God intended. They walked with God every day. They talked openly with him, laughed with him, and completely enjoyed the wonder of the world he built for them. They had a perfect relationship with God and with each other. They had a perfect environment, a perfect job, a perfect climate—and God called it all "very good."

Jesus also enjoyed a perfect relationship with his Father while he was on earth. He heard his voice, enjoyed his presence, and walked completely in his love and sovereignty. One of the most astonishing blessings of Jesus's atoning sacrifice on Calvary is that he restored the opportunity for you and me to again enjoy a daily, moment-by-moment walk with our Father.

Here are but a few of the many scriptures that tell us of the Father-heart of God:

> If you, then, though you are evil, know how to give good gifts to your children, *how much more will your Father in heaven give good gifts to those who ask him!* Matthew 7:11

> So the son got up and went to his father. But *while he was still a long way off, his father saw him and was filled with compassion* for him; *he ran to his son, threw his arms around him and kissed him.* And the father said to his servants, "Quick! Bring the best robe and put it on him. Put a ring on his finger and sandals on his feet. Bring the fattened calf and kill it. Let's have a feast and celebrate." Luke 15:20, 22, 23, 31

> Jesus said, "The *Father Himself loves you* because you have loved me and have believed that I came from God." John 16:27

> For you did not receive a spirit that makes you a slave again to fear, but *you received the Spirit of sonship. And by him we cry, "Abba, Father."* Romans 8:15

> For I am convinced that neither death nor life, neither angels nor demons, neither the present nor the future, nor any powers, neither height nor depth, nor anything else in all creation, will be *able to separate us from the love of God* that is in Christ Jesus our Lord. Romans 8:38–39

The Bottom Line?

1. We are all personally hand-crafted by a loving Father in his image.

2. We are significant. Our lives matter.

3. He breathed his life into us and made us each a "living soul."

4. We are made to enjoy an intimate, daily, personal relationship with him.

5. Because of Jesus's sacrifice, we can enjoy such a relationship now.

There is an experience of the love of God which, when it comes upon us, and enfolds us, and bathes us, and warms us, is so utterly new that we can hardly identify it with the old phrase, God is love. Can this be the love of God, this burning, tender, wooing, wounding pain of love that pierces the marrow of my bones and burns out old loves and ambitions—God experienced, is a vast surprise.
~Thomas R. Kelly

The Heart of God— for "husband"

Adam had a good thing going. He enjoyed a perfect relationship with the Creator God. He lived in a magnificent garden, made by God. He had a perfect job (caretaker and *husband*man of the garden), perfect weather, perfect food, and perfect health —everything that a man could possibly want.

> The Lord God took the man and put him in the Garden of Eden to *work it and take care of it.* Genesis 2:15

Just what was Adam doing as a "*husband*man," caretaker, steward? God placed Adam in a role of responsibility. He was the manager, the protector, the shepherd of this most awesome and beautiful place. The verb "husband" is defined in this way: "to direct and manage with frugality; to use or employ in the manner best suited to produce the greatest effect."

Isn't it interesting that God created man and immediately put him to work in the garden? It is hard for us to think of work in its original form, rather than the post-Fall, cursed, sweat-of-your-brow kind of work. For Adam, work was awesome. He partnered with God in a fabulous environment and used his newfound skills to make things grow and flourish. He wanted what he did to please God. He took great delight in what he was given to do. Adam was created and wired (as are we all) to *do* something important, significant, and lasting. As men, we are prewired to be stewards, caretakers of God's creation—"husbands."

The Bible doesn't tell us how long Adam lived in the garden by himself, but it must have taken quite some time to name all the animals. During that process, it became painfully obvious to Adam that all the other creatures had mates. They were all experiencing life with someone "like them." Adam saw animals mating and watched with wonder as young animals were born and families were created.

God was also watching, and he knew that "it is not good for man to be alone."

So, in God's sovereign love and wisdom, he created a fifty-two-inch, flat-screen, high-def television for Adam to watch.

Or was it a shiny new Harley Davidson for Adam's enjoyment? Maybe a brand new set of golf clubs? A chocolate Lab puppy? A new 4x4 truck?

Thankfully, the scriptures say:

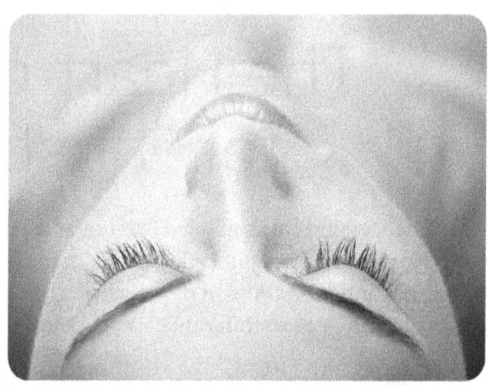

The man gave names to all the cattle, and to the birds of the sky, and to every beast of the field, but for Adam there was not found a helper suitable for him. So the Lord God caused a deep sleep to fall upon the man, and he slept; then He took one of his ribs and closed up the flesh at that place.

The Lord God fashioned into a woman the rib which He had taken from the man, and brought her to the man.

The man said,

"This is now bone of my bones, And flesh of my flesh;
She shall be called Woman,Because she was taken out of Man."

For this reason a man shall leave his father and his mother, and be joined to his *wife*; and they shall become one flesh. *Genesis 2:20–24*

The Almighty, Creator God, who loved Adam like no other created thing, knew that there was only one thing that would satisfy the deepest need in Adam's soul—woman.

1. The rest of me

Adam was obviously ecstatic. He was no longer "single." Finally, there was another creature "like" himself. The verb tense in scripture tells us that Adam literally shouted. He exclaimed, "Finally," at last—*this* is who I've been longing for!

He was also well aware that this "woman" came from him. God chose not to create her from "the dust of the ground," like Adam. This beautiful creature was literally formed using a part of Adam's body. She was really made from "bone of his bone, and flesh of his flesh." This implies inseparable unity. This is the only way Eve could be directly related to Adam apart from childbirth. She was part of him. She was, in a sense, the rest of him. He was now complete.

2. A divine mystery

It is very interesting to note that Adam not only enjoyed a perfect external environment, but he also, more than any human ever, enjoyed moment-by-moment fellowship with God himself. He literally walked and talked with God all day long.

Yet, there was still something missing in Adam's heart and soul. Something that not even his relationship with God could fill. Somehow God created a personal need, void, longing in the heart of man and woman that can only be met through an earthly relationship between a husband and wife. Eve was not just a fellow human or a close female friend. Genesis 2:22 clearly indicates more than just a personal introduction—this was Adam and Eve's marriage (evidenced by the words *wife* and *husband* from this point onward).

God has chosen to mysteriously meet certain needs in a man's life through an imperfect, challenging, ever-mystifying relationship with his wife.

3. Joined to his wife

Genesis 2:24 addresses three very important issues:

1. Man is to "leave his father and mother and be joined to his wife." In this context, the word leave means "severance." God's plan is for the husband to establish a family unit in a new location. This is partly to fulfill his command to "fill the earth and subdue it" (Genesis 1:28) and partly to emphasize that marriage involves two people who are mature enough to establish a new home without parental supervision and support.

2. The concept of being "joined" means permanence. It is God's intention that the husband-wife relationship (marriage) last for a lifetime. When discussing marriage with the religious leaders of his day, Jesus stressed this point also:

"Haven't you read," he replied, "that at the beginning the Creator 'made them male and female,' and said, 'For this reason a man will leave his father and mother and be united to his wife, and the two will become one flesh'? So they are no longer two, but one. Therefore what God has joined together, let no one (man-human) separate." *Matthew 19:4–6*

Jesus states another important point about the marriage relationship—therefore, what God has joined together. Marriage is a sacred covenant before God, and he is the one who knits a couple together. Marriage is intended to be a living representation of the covenant-keeping love Christ has for his bride, the church. Staying married is not just about staying in love; it is about staying in (keeping) covenant with one another.

3. "And they shall become one flesh." As one flesh through marriage, Adam and Eve became greater as one than they had been as separate individuals. We read in Genesis that when Adam was alone, his singular mission was to be the caretaker and steward of God's marvelous garden. After God brought Adam and Eve together in marriage, God told them to "be fruitful and increase in number; fill the earth and subdue it." Together, they had a much bigger mission and job than Adam had alone.

Also, the fact that Eve was formed from a rib taken out of Adam's side (Genesis 2:21–22) makes it very clear that Adam and Eve were both literally and physically "one flesh." There is no stronger evidence than this that in marriage, two really become one.

Anyone who has been happily married for twenty, thirty, or forty years will tell you that over time, husbands and wives begin to think alike, sound alike, enjoy the same things, and complete each others' sentences. Many even begin to look alike.

One of the goals of a lifetime of marriage is to "become one." It doesn't happen on the honeymoon, and it doesn't happen without a lifetime of giving, serving, loving, and yielding to God's will and direction for our personal lives—and our marriages.

A good marriage is the union of two forgivers.
~ Ruth Bell Graham

4. "Husband" of another kind

As we have discussed, Adam had the awesome responsibility and pleasure of partnering with God as the caretaker, steward, manager, and husband of God's Garden of Delight. Every day he talked with God, walked with God, and was the beneficiary of God's personal attention, love, encouragement, and wisdom. How cool would that have been?

Think about this with me—God is so wise, so sovereign, so loving that he knew what was up the road for Adam. He knew that Adam would have a wife, a special woman, who would need someone to "husband" her also. So, instead of making Adam a cowboy, fisherman, or carpenter, he trained him, in advance, to be a skilled steward and caretaker—a *husband*.

God knew that the woman he created would have unique needs, and he knew that Adam (with God's help) would be able to fill those needs. What a wonderful God!

God has wired men with God-given husbanding skills. He has also designed our wives to be so amazingly complex that we must seek God's help in utilizing those skills. He never intended for marriage to be lived apart from his presence, involvement, and oversight. Without his personal involvement, we are left to our own wisdom, ideas, and best-guess efforts to make marriage work. And as we saw at the beginning of this book, we are not doing a very good job of that.

We are wired to be husbands. God supplies all the resources we need to do our job well. We can't, however, do that job without him.

5. By Him and for Him

> *For by him all things were created: things in heaven and on earth, visible and invisible, whether thrones or powers or rulers or authorities; all things were created by him and for him. He is before all things, and in him all things hold together. Colossians 1:16–17*

Marriage, like everything else God designed, was created by him and for him. God created marriage for his glory. A man and a wife, living in harmony with God and each other, bring much glory to God. The primary spiritual purpose of any marriage is to be a shining illustration of his unconditional, covenant love to the world.

Because two naturally selfish people living in a lifetime commitment is extraordinarily hard, marriage was also created to draw us into a greater dependence on, and intimacy with, God himself. Like Jesus, we are totally dependent on God's power, wisdom, patience, grace, and love to stay in a fulfilling relationship with the same woman – for a lifetime.

The Bottom Line

1. We all have soul needs that God chose not to completely fill.

2. Our spouse is uniquely designed to complete us and meet those needs.

3. God created our wife and marriage as marvelous gifts for us.

4. God created marriage to be a reflection of his glory.

5. Marriage is designed to be a covenant relationship—a permanent commitment.

6. Marriage is God's mirror to show us what is really in our hearts and how we are making progress in our walk with him.

7. Like Jesus (John 15:5), we can do nothing without him.

Your marriage will be as fulfilling
as is your walk with Jesus
~ Rob Thorpe

What went wrong?

If marriage is such a wonderful, fulfilling, permanent thing – why are so many ending in heartache, separation, and divorce?

I have to tell you that my wife and I asked that very question after attending our twenty-year high school reunion. We discovered that out of our high school graduating class, which numbered more than 350, we were one of a very small group who were still married to their first spouses.

Depending on the source of the research, approximately 50 percent of first marriages in the United States will end in divorce. According to the Forest Institute of Professional Psychology and the Enrichment Journal and the National Center for Health Statistics, more than 60 percent of second marriages and more than 70 percent of third marriages end in divorce.

According to well-known researcher George Barna's March 2008 study, Americans who call themselves Christians fare only slightly better at 46 percent. So, what's the deal? What went wrong?

I hope by now you more fully understand the heart of God for marriage. He created marriage as a blessing to fulfill us beyond our wildest dreams. Like everything else he created, it was perfect. That was obviously before the Fall of Adam and Eve in the Garden.

As we know from reading Genesis 2 and 3, God loves us enough to give us free will. He gives us the freedom to choose to love, obey, and follow him or to follow our own ways. Sadly, Adam and Eve chose to turn their backs on God and his goodness and live independently of him. As a result, God had to banish them from his perfectly created garden environment and allow them to venture out into a world apart from God's continual presence and blessing.

> And the Lord God said, "The man has now become like one of us, knowing good and evil. He must not be allowed to reach out his hand and take also from the tree of life and eat, and live forever." So the Lord God banished him from the Garden of Eden to work the ground from which he had been taken. After he drove them out, he placed on the east side of the Garden of Eden cherubim and a flaming sword flashing back and forth to guard the way to the tree of life. *Genesis 3:22 –24*

It is into this world that each of us has been born ever since. Here are a few passages that describe the culture in which we live:

> I have come as Light into the world, so that everyone who believes in Me will not remain in darkness. *John 12:46*

> For He (Jesus) rescued us from the domain of darkness, and transferred us to the kingdom of His beloved Son. *Colossians 1:13*

> Therefore, just as through one man sin entered into the world, and death through sin, and so death spread to all men, because all sinned. *Romans 5:12*

> But I see a different law in the members of my body, waging war against the law of my mind and making me a prisoner of the law of sin which is in my members. *Romans 7:23*

> In whose case the god of this world has blinded the minds of the unbelieving so that they might not see the light of the gospel of the glory of Christ, who is the image of God. *2 Corinthians 4:4*

Because we are born into a world of darkness, selfishness, and sin, it's no wonder that marriage is another casualty of our human condition. When you take two self-focused, "me-absorbed" people and put them together—and apply the pressures of life, work, finances, children, in-laws, etc.—*boom*! It is amazing that even more marriages don't end in divorce.

> ***The force of selfishness is as inevitable and as calculable as the force of gravitation.***
> ***~ Hailliard***

> *None are so empty as those who are full of themselves.*
> *~ Benjamin Whichcote*

By nature, each of us is a self-focused, "life is about me" person. When my firstborn son began to talk, some of his first words were "mine," "me do it," and "no." We don't have to be taught how to be selfish. We are born that way. We want what we want when we want it. It is our natural condition. Much like a default setting on a computer, each morning we wake up and our setting is ME. We default to a mindset and lifestyle that centers on our own wants, needs, and agendas.

Ever since Adam and Eve chose to disobey God and turn their backs on his love and leadership, man has been born into a world of self-absorption. We feel it is our goal in life, even our inalienable right, to be happy. We want to do what makes us happy.

When asked why marriage is so hard, Dr. Steven Stosny answered with another question:

> For whom is marriage hard? Marriage is only hard for those who:
>
> - Try to make their partners into someone they are not
> - Believe they have superior rights, tastes, preferences, beliefs, or morality
> - Are unwilling to see their partner's perspectives alongside their own
> - Are convinced that their partners are selfish, incompatible, or defective
> - Are unwilling to admire their partners' strengths and regard their vulnerabilities with compassion and support
> - Are unwilling to appreciate the value and meaning their partner's add to their lives.
>
> If you are one of those people, marriage will seem impossible.

Notice the inferences in the statements above:

1. *I* want my spouse to be who *I* need her to be.
2. *My* rights, tastes, expectations, preferences, etc. are more important than my spouse's.
3. Unlike my wife, *my* perspective is right.
4. *I* have concluded that my spouse is selfish (luckily, I am not).
5. *I* am too focused on meeting *my* own needs to notice my spouse's.
6. Since life is about *me*, *I* cannot appreciate someone else's value.

Dr. Stosny's conclusions tell only part of the story. The main storyline, however, is that we are, by nature, selfish. We have wants and needs, and it is the duty of our spouses to meet them! Right?

Life Happens …

Most couples begin to realize during their engagements that they have profound differences. He loves football; she couldn't care less. She wants to talk about everything; he tends to internalize things. She likes to shop; he likes to save. The list goes on and on. They're so much in love and so excited about being married that they overlook these differences and even joke about them.

During the honeymoon, these and other traits become a little more noticeable, but hey, love is blind. Right?

Then, after coming home, life hits them in the face. The honeymoon was wonderful, but now they have jobs, meals, laundry, bills, school, budgets, etc. This is when those cute little differences begin to become irritating—like a pebble in your shoe during a long walk. These differences can become real, annoying issues and pressure points in a marriage. It is amazing how quickly our blindness is cured, and we begin to notice things we hadn't seen before.

All three of my wonderful sons are now married, and they each told me early in their marriages that they love being married but that it is "hard." Yes, it is hard. We are selfish and find it very difficult to subordinate our wants and needs to anyone else, no matter how much we love them.

As we have already seen, marriage was created by God to be perfect in every way—a relationship of complete oneness and blissful fulfillment. But, there was a fall. With the fall came sin, hardship, and life apart from God's perfect plan. Marriage became hard.

There is an interesting verse in 1 Corinthians that offers a realistic view of marriage: "But if you do marry, you have not sinned; and if a virgin marries, she has not sinned. But those who marry will face many troubles in this life. *1 Corinthians 7:28*

Keep in mind that the primary goal of marriage is not to make us happy. The goal of marriage is to further conform us to the image of God and to bring him glory. The troubles promised in the verse above are not meant to weigh us down or cause us pain and heartache but to draw us close to God and to each other and to bring him glory in the way we handle them.

The older I get, the more I realize that there are always areas in my life that need attention. When things are good at home, things seem to be crazy at work. When work is going well, my wife and I aren't hitting on all cylinders. When the wife and I are doing great, it seems close friends or family members are in real need. Then, when everything seems to be running well, my family is hit with a financial need.

Is God out to get us?
Is he mad at us?
Have we done something to warrant his wrath?
The answer is none of the above.

The Heart of God—for You

One of the most amazing truths of the Bible and most endearing characteristics of our Father God is this: ***There is nothing you can do to make Him love you more, and there is nothing you can do to make Him love you less.***

He loves you. He likes you. There is nothing that you have ever done, or will ever do, to change that!

What is God Like?
by Doug Sherman (with permission)

He is the most decent person you will ever meet. He is relentlessly affectionate, loving, honest, sincere, caring, and with perfect integrity. There is nothing in Him that is not good. He has never done an unkind thing and never will. No bad intentions or bad thoughts exist in Him, only perfect goodness.

His only motive for His commandments is for our well-being and pleasure. He is perfectly fair in how He judges. He is perfectly truthful in all He says. He is perfectly compassionate and gracious toward those in need. He is monumentally kind. His plan for your life is brilliant. He will magnify the results of the good things you do and even turn bad decisions into good results over time.

Every act is perfect. He makes no mistakes and is competent to run not only the universe but also your life and mine. No purpose or plan of His can be stopped. He is courageous and He lives an infinitely high and noble purpose every moment of eternity. He is completely consistent in His character. He is the best Listener you have ever met. He is a Rescuer whose nature is to save those in trouble. He is the kindest and most gracious Person who ever lived. He is the smartest Person in the universe. There is nothing He does not know and He cannot learn anything, because He knows it all. He feels angry at evil, He is grieved by pain and suffering, He feels compassion toward the weak, He takes great pleasure in His people.

He is the happiest Person in the universe with the sunniest disposition. He is perfectly happy in who He is, what He does, and in His relationship with the other members of the Trinity.

He is a perfect Father in His loving affection for His children. He is a perfect King with benevolent desires for His people to provide for them and protect them. He is a perfect Friend whose loyalty is infinite and who longs to live life with you every moment.

He is a jealous Lover who longs for you to find Him the most attractive thing in your heart and to love Him with all your heart, mind, soul and strength. He is a perfect Shepherd longing to bless you, lead and protect you and give you the desires of His heart.

It is an astounding truth that we were created in His image. This means we have a heart that is a miniature of His. We were built to be happy, generous, courageous, merciful and kind. We were given a passion for what is right and noble and just. We are designed with a heart that hates evil and the desire to rescue others from it.

Being made in the image of God, we are fully loved and are able to fully love. We are created to experience life to the fullest, to laugh and have fun, to commune with him and to do significant and important things. We are created to be joyful and to enjoy a most intimate union with God. We are created for his glory. Hard to believe, isn't it? God not only loves you, but he also likes you and wants to hang out with you.

He has great plans for you, and he can't wait to show you all he has in store.

> "For I know the plans I have for you," declares the Lord, "plans to prosper you and not to harm you, plans to give you hope and a future." *Jeremiah 29:11*
>
> For we are God's workmanship, created in Christ Jesus to do good works, which God prepared in advance for us to do. *Ephesians 2:10*

> Command those who are rich in this present world not to be arrogant nor to put their hope in wealth, which is so uncertain, but to put their hope in God, who richly provides us with everything for our enjoyment. *1 Timothy 6:17*

On September 9, 2008, The Washington Post published a remarkable story written by a well-known movie writer.

Joe Eszterhas
My Base Instincts and God's Love

Seven years ago, I sat down on a curb near my home, sobbing, and asked God to help me.
I had just had surgery for throat cancer. I still had a trache in my throat. I had been told that if I didn't stop smoking and drinking immediately, I'd die. I desperately didn't want to die. I adored my wife and children.

But I knew I couldn't stop. I'd started smoking when I was twelve 12 and drinking when I was 14. I was now 57 years old.

I cried and begged God to help me … and He did. I hadn't prayed since I was a boy. I had made fun of God and those who loved God in my writings. And now, through my sobs, I heard myself asking God to help me … and from the moment I asked, He did.

I didn't at first understand why He did. I didn't deserve His help, I thought. I was unworthy. I ignore Him for forty years and then suddenly I ask Him to help me and He does? It took me some time to understand that God helped me because He loves me. Because even though we don't deserve God's love, God loves us—all - all of us.

Not only did He give me the strength to be able to defeat my addictions, He saved my life. My throat surgeon, Dr. Marshall Strome, told me seven years after the surgery that I am "cured." Not that I am in remission, but that I am cured. That my throat tissue has regenerated so remarkably that even a doctor examining my throat wouldn't be able to tell that there was ever cancer there. Dr. Strome, who had removed about eighty percent of my larynx, called this "a miracle."

I call it that, too. Why did God save the life of a man who had trashed, lampooned, and marginalized Him most of his life? Why did He take the time and the trouble to save me? It certainly wasn't because I had written Basic Instinct and Showgirls, right? Was it because my wife and I had four little boys we were trying to raise? Possibly.

Or was it God's divinely impish sense of humor? "Who, you? You're praying? After everything you've done to break my commandments and after every nasty, unfunny thing you've written about Me and those who follow Me—now - now you're sobbing? Praying? Asking Me to help you? Hah! Okay, fine, I'll help you. But if I do, know this: My help will obliterate the old, infamous you. You'll wind up turning your life inside-out. You'll wind up stopping all of your excesses. You know what will happen to you? You'll wind up telling the world what I did for you. You'll wind up carrying my cross in church. Yes, I make all things new—and - and you will be new, too."

Well, I thought I heard God saying all those things to me … and then all of the things God said would happen … did. My life has turned inside-out. I have stopped my excesses and replaced them with prayer and long walks. I am carrying the cross as often as they'll let me at Holy Angels Church in Bainbridge Township, Ohio. And I have written a book as a thank-you to God. Not just for saving my life, but for saving me.

I am witness to and the beneficiary of God's love for all of us. Am I am witness, too, to the fact that His love is so strong that it was even able to open my rusty old closed heart.

I will thank Him forever because He gave me new life and a heart which is truly able to love for the first time in my life. His love is mine.

Joe Eszterhas is the author of a new memoir called "Crossbearer." He has written the screenplays for sixteen films, totaling over $1 billion in box office revenue. His blockbusters include Basic Instinct, Jagged Edge, Flashdance and Showgirls. A former senior editor at Rolling Stone, he is the author of five previous books—the - the second, "Charlie Simpson's Apocalypse," was nominated for the National Book Award.

God really does know us. He really does love us. Joe experienced God's personal and overpowering love first hand.

The Bottom Line

1. Because of Adam and Eve's sin, we are all born into a world of *self*.

2. Self-focused people make poor marriage partners.

3. Life's troubles are designed by a sovereign God to draw us closer to him.

4. God loves us, no matter what.

5. Understanding God's unconditional, passionate love for us is the foundation of all other relationships in our life, especially marriage.

Then Christ will make his home in your hearts as you trust in him. Your roots will grow down into God's love and keep you strong. And may you have the power to understand, as all God's people should, how wide, how long, how high, and how deep his love is. May you experience the love of Christ, though it is too great to understand fully. Then you will be made complete with all the fullness of life and power that comes from God.

~Ephesians 3:17-19 NLT

Part 2

What Do I Do with This?

So, if marriage is designed by a loving Father God to fulfill me in ways that nothing else and no one else can, what must I do? What does he require of me in order to experience marriage as God intended and to be the husband I'm supposed to be?

> *I am satisfied that, when the Almighty wants me to do, or not to do, a particular thing, He finds a way of letting me know it*
> *~ Abraham Lincoln*

Men, by nature, want to "do" something or "fix" things. If we have a problem, let's fix it and move on. Fortunately, God doesn't offer us a magic pill or three-step formula to fix our lives and marriages. What he does give us is his perfect wisdom, his intimate presence, and his empowering Spirit. Believe me, we need all three to succeed.

Because man was created first, he is given the primary role of leadership in the home. This weighty responsibility is purposely designed by God, and he has given us specific instructions, wisdom, and strength to fulfill that appointed role. Hundreds of books have been written on being a better husband. As I said before, this is not another self-help book. In my opinion, the bottom line on being the husbands God calls us to be comes from his word. Who better to tell us what is expected and what will produce great results than the creator of marriage himself?

While most of the following verses are written specifically to husbands, I include others that are written about relationships in general.
Let's dive in.

The Bible ... God's Word or Suggestions for Living?

Is it God's word or not?

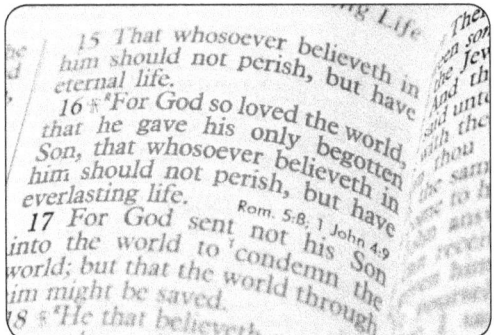

How you answer that question will have a lot to do with how you respond to this book. If the Bible is God's actual word to us and is to be obeyed, you will have one response. If it is merely man's written thoughts and only contains good principles for living, then your response will be quite different.

It is my deeply held belief that the Bible is truly God's word. If God said it, it is true. If God says do it, it must be good, and I better be about the business of doing it. If I don't do it, I am deliberately disobeying and am choosing to sin. Thus, if what I have said so far is correct, then God's word regarding marriage is his loving and wise instruction, intended to equip us to more fully experience his design for an abundantly fulfilling marriage.

If you are reading this book and don't have a personal relationship with the God of the universe, the Father who created you and the author of marriage, I pray that you will take a minute to read the following scriptures and ask the most loving person in the universe—Jesus—to become the king and ruler of your life (and marriage) from this point forward.

> That if you confess with your mouth, "Jesus is Lord," and believe in your heart that God raised him from the dead, you will be saved. *Romans 10:9*

> For, "Everyone who calls on the name of the Lord will be saved." *Romans 10:13*

> For it is by grace you have been saved, through faith—and this not from yourselves, it is the gift of God. *Ephesians 2:8*

If you are struggling in your marriage and sincerely seeking help, please know that God can and will change you and your marriage if you let him.

Since only God has the real answers and only he can provide the desire and the power to change us, it only makes sense to turn to him for wisdom and advice. He created you and me, he created our wives, and he created marriage. He knows what is wrong and how to go about fixing it.

God's Word Specifically to Husbands

This section highlights scripture specifically written to husbands. In all fairness, there are plenty of Bible verses aimed at wives also, so don't feel picked on.

What follows does not come from a seminar or a television show. These are not the words of a pastor, author, counselor, or friend. What follows are God's Words. They are the bottom line when it comes to knowing what "husbands" are to do within the marriage relationship. These are not God's suggestions for your consideration. These are commandments, and they carry just as much weight as thou shall not kill, commit adultery, or steal.

You may have read these verses many times before, but if you are not acting on them or obeying what God says in them, you are not obeying God. You cannot be the husband you want to be or develop oneness with God or your wife if you are willfully turning your back on what he says. As you read ahead, ask him to make his words come alive to you, to convict you of self-centeredness in your own heart, and to change you. He wants to. He can. He will.
Here are two key verses to ponder before we launch into some of these familiar verses and passages:

> John 13:17: "If you know these things, you are blessed if you do them."

> James 4:17: "If you don't do what you know is right, you have sinned."

I Corinthians 7:2–5

> *But since there is so much immorality, each man should have his own wife, and each woman her own husband. The husband should fulfill his marital duty to his wife, and likewise the wife to her husband. The wife's body does not belong to her alone but also to her husband. In the same way, the husband's body does not belong to him alone but also to his wife. Do not deprive each other except by mutual consent and for a time, so that you may devote yourselves to prayer. Then come together again so that Satan will not tempt you because of your lack of self-control.*

The original language provides us with more insight into the author's intention contained in these verses:

Each ... should have. The Greek word *echo* means "to have, possess continually." The marriage relationship is the only legitimate place for sexual expression. The marriage relationship is God's primary provision for your sexual drives and their complete expression and satisfaction. Because of sexual immorality, God wants you to have your own wife. Not someone else's wife and not multiple wives, but "your own" wife.

Wife ... husband. Any fulfillment of your sexual needs outside of your wife is not the will of the Lord. She is your only avenue of sexual pleasure. She is your God-given solution.

Body does not belong. This is the bottom line principle regarding sex within marriage. God created sex as a shared experience between a husband and wife.

Deprive. Greek *apostereo* means "to deprive, wrong, or defraud another of what belongs to him." Sex between husband and wife is a right and responsibility that must not be withheld except by mutual consent, because the spouse's body does not belong to him/her alone but also to his/her spouse. The grammar used here also asserts that sex, or withholding sex, must not be a tool to control your spouse!

So that ... Satan will not tempt you because of your lack of self-control. Paul, the writer of 1 Corinthians, recognizes that a strong sex drive can lead to fornication and adultery if it is not satisfied within marriage, especially if there has not been sufficient development of self-control before marriage (see 1 Corinthians 7:9). Even though married, a spouse may still fall to Satan's temptation if the spouse has not developed self-control or is being "deprived" in marriage.

Even married couples need to be extremely careful of Satan's insidious lies and temptations within marriage. Human sexuality, though a precious gift from God, is a powerful human drive. Satan uses this strong biological need as a tool to alienate men from God and from their wives.

Paul tells us that there will be dire consequences if we drop the ball regarding these verses. Satan will severely tempt you in sexual areas such as pornography, lust, masturbation, and flirtation. The resulting devastation will cause severe pain and death to your soul, your relationships, and your witness for Christ. This is precisely Satan's plan for us (see John 10:9–10), and believe me, Satan is much better at tempting than you are at resisting. He has had centuries of practice.

Don't be naïve either; your wife craves affirmation, praise, and validation from you, her husband. She longs for a deep, emotional closeness and responsiveness from you. For her, this is the art of sex. It is not about sexual release and physical relief. If she does not receive these things from you, she will be tempted also to look elsewhere for fulfillment (soap operas, romance novels, hobbies, Internet friends, or even another man).

Let's break this down into bite-sized pieces:

We husbands are to a) fulfill our marital duty to our wives sexually (emotionally), and b) remember that our bodies do not belong to us alone sexually, *and* …

I am going to take a little license here and expound on the whole idea of a husband's body not belonging to himself alone but to his wife also. We just discussed what that means sexually in the Bible, but I want to offer some additional food for thought. After thirty-five years of marriage, I have discovered how this idea carries over into all areas of my marriage.

Think with me about some of the other, nonsexual parts of your body and how they should be your wife's also:

My Body
It may sound silly, but my body, my physical presence, should be available to my wife. I should fight to make time to be with her. Do I spend more time at the office or enjoying hobbies than I do with her? When I am home, am I with her or zoning out in front of a mind-numbing football game? I need to think about how my body can serve her by taking out the trash, caring for the yard, keeping the cars clean and serviced, helping with cooking/cleaning, etc. You get the picture. Does my wife have access to my body to lighten her burdens in life?

My Brain
Does my mind stay so occupied with my to-do list at work, my upcoming fishing trip, my agenda, my goals, etc. that I have little or no time to think about my wife and her needs, goals, and dreams? Do I really listen when she talks to me about her day, the kids, or her conversations with friends and family, or am I mentally tapping my foot and hoping this all ends soon? Do I have any brain space available to just think about what a God-ordained blessing she is to me and what I can do when I get home from work to show her I love and appreciate her?

My Eyes
Do I really look at my wife when I speak to her? (She knows I am really listening when I do.) Do I only have eyes for her, or do I eagerly gaze at attractive women when she is not around? Do I secretly view pornography, whether online or in movies, to meet some unfulfilled need in my soul and then feel the weight of guilt and shame when I am with my wife?

My Mouth
Is my mouth available to her? Do I make the phone call that she hates to make to a friend, relative, or repairman? Does my mouth show her proper respect and remind her often of my deep love for her? How good am I at encouraging her and making her feel significant in my life? Do I ask her sincere questions or only talk about me and my interests? Do I pray out loud for her and in her presence?

My Ears
When I hear my wife call for me, do I get up quickly to help or do I say, "After this play, Honey" or "Can't it wait until the commercial?" Do I actively listen to her when she talks? Do I take delight in helping her talk through her life issues, or do I mentally rush ahead to "fix" the problem?

My Hands and Feet
Does she have complete use of my hands and feet? And, yes, this involves getting up from my favorite chair. Do I resent walking around an outlet mall in search of the perfect gift or the "I can't believe how much we saved" bargain? Do I resent having to help her unload groceries or, heaven forbid, actually going with her to the grocery store on my sacred Saturday?

My Heart
Is she still the love of my life? Am I doing anything to show her? Do I have other loves in my heart that compete for my affections—work hobbies, possessions, other women (actual or imaginary)? Am I giving away pieces of my heart and my affection by flirting with other women at work or in Internet chat rooms?
I hope you catch the drift by now. Your body is not yours alone but your wife's also. We need to continually ask ourselves and God if we are making our bodies and all their parts available to our wives.

Speaking of Sex...

Let's just go ahead and say it—our wives "just don't get it." I can't tell you how many times I have heard a sexually frustrated husband say these words. And the truth is that she really doesn't.

That's because she can't. God did not design her the same way. Her sexual desires and stimuli are vastly different from yours. Science has proven that men have physical needs from sex that are not the same in women. Our ductwork is such that we need sexual release (climax) more often, or we get very "edgy." The Bible is also very clear that our wives are to be the only legitimate outlet for this release. This tension in marriage causes incredible conflict, stress, and heartache.

One of the Seminars we have created at Square1Ministries^{sm}, called "The Sex Talk", is designed to help wives and husbands better understand the psychology and physiology that is so very difficult them to discuss without seeming extremely self-serving.

In a nutshell, here are some of the high points from the seminar:

Men:

1. Have a strong, God-given physical/biological need for sexual release/relief and are wired to initiate sex.
2. Desire a wife's responsiveness—affirmation, wanted, desired, needed, loved, and respected.
3. Desire physical closeness—liked, friendship, and shared recreational experiences.
4. Have a strong visual gateway—primary sex organ. We care about our wife's appearance.
5. Are easily bored—desire adventure, risk, variety, challenge; bore with routine, predictable sex. We want to be wanted and desired; we want her to "want to."

Our wives have equally valid and strong emotional needs which God expects us to uncover, appreciate and meet also. Take the time to discover what those are, and how you can fulfill them. Remember – "he who loves his wife, loves himself".

I Corinthians 7: 33

> *But a married man is concerned about the affairs of this world—how he can please his wife.*

In this context, the wording Paul uses refers to the normal affairs of married life that compete with our time and energy for the Lord.

A married man has a family to provide for, a wife to please, and job to perform well—not to mention his own hobbies, ministries, interests, and goals.

Paul's thoughts also point to a very important message that husbands need to grasp: the primary concern in this world for a husband should be how to please his wife!

Yes, work is important. You are responsible to "bring home the bacon." Your role as a father is critical. And then there are all those crucial ministries you are involved in at church. They are all very important roles. But in God's eyes, the *most* important affair of this world—your *most* important calling beyond loving and pleasing him—is to please your wife.

Back to sexual intimacy - Researchers at the University of Chicago recently declared that 75% of men reach orgasm during intercourse while only 33% of women. Even in this most crucial area of oneness and connection – we still put ourselves first.

Can we honestly say that "pleasing our wives" is the most important goal on our daily to-do lists?

Ephesians 5: 21, 23, 25–33

> **For the husband is the head of the wife *as Christ* is the head of the church, his body, of which he is the Savior.** *Ephesians 5:23*

Christ is depicted as the husband and the church as the bride (cf. Rev. 19:7; 21:2, 9). Husbands need to act in their God-given leadership position just as Christ did. He gave himself up for the church. This is not an issue of control, but of sacrifice. He gave his time, his energy, and his very life for his bride, and she (the church) didn't deserve it either!

"But you don't know *my* wife." The bottom line is that it doesn't matter. Christ loved us and gave himself up for us when "we were dead in our trespasses and sins" (Eph. 2:1-5). Jesus continues to love us unconditionally—no matter what. He expects us to love our wives in the same way. There are no excuses.
Why? Because marriage is a living parable of Christ and his church. Our marriages represent Christ and his love and devotion to us—his bride.

> **Husbands, *love your wives*, just *as Christ loved the church* and *gave himself* up for her (on her behalf) to make her holy, cleansing her by the washing with water through the word, and to present her to himself as a radiant church, without stain or wrinkle or any other blemish, but holy and blameless. In this same way, husbands ought to *love their wives as their own bodies*. He who *loves his wife* loves himself. After all, no one ever hated his own body, but *he feeds and cares for* it, just as Christ does the church—for we are members of his body. "For this reason a man will leave his father and mother and be united to his wife, and the two will become one flesh." This is a profound mystery—but I am talking about Christ and the church. However, each one of you also *must love his wife* as he loves himself, and the wife must respect her husband. - Ephesians 5:25–33**

As husbands, we should set the spiritual atmosphere in our homes by continuing to love our wives as Christ loved the church. Christian husbands are servant leaders, not bosses.

In light of the fact that wives are commanded to submit to their husbands, we might think that God would then command men to rule well over their wives and families. Instead, husbands are commanded to love their wives. Paul uses the same Greek word for love (*agapao*) that is used to express the kind of love God feels for us and that compelled him to send his only begotten son into the world to die as the penalty for our sins (John 3:16).

It is a self-sacrificing type of love that is spiritual in nature. Paul makes a direct correlation between the love Christ has for us and the love husbands are to give their wives.

> *"The Christian is supposed to love his neighbor,*
> *and since his wife is his nearest neighbor,*
> *she should be his deepest love."*
> *~ Martin Luther*

> *"The real act of marriage takes place in the heart,*
> *not in the ballroom or church or synagogue.*
> *It's a choice you make - not just on your*
> *wedding day, but over and over again."*
> *~ Barbara de Angelis*

Ten Ways Christ Loves His Church (From the Book of John)

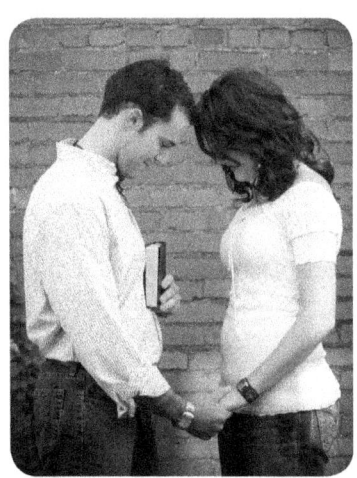

- He protects her from evil influences (world, Satan). *John 2:13–15*
- He shows her, by example, how to walk with God. *John 5:19, 30; 6:38*
- He provides for her physical needs. *John 6:10–14*
- He forgives her offenses without condemnation or shame. *John 8:3–11*
- He shepherds (leads, protects, provides for) her. *John 10:11, 28*
- He lays down his life for her. *John 10:15, 18; 13:18–19*
- He knows her (needs, fears, dreams). *John 10:14*
- He humbles himself to serve her. *John 13:3–17*
- He prays for her. *John 17*
- He never leaves her. *John 20–21; see also Acts 2*

What Does That Look Like—for Me?

Jesus Christ is the perfect example of what it means to be a *husband* and how to love a wife in a sacrificial way. What does it mean for a husband to lay down his life for his wife? Laying down your life involves consciously making daily choices to serve your wife and family.
These choices don't just happen. They are the result of becoming "deliberate" in your approach to being a husband. Ask yourself:

- Am I adding to or lightening my wife's burdens?
- How am I doing in helping/serving around the house (not reluctantly but with joy)?
- Am I being a servant when it comes to rearing and disciplining our children?
- Am I loving her like Christ by being sensitive to her needs?
- Do I even know what her needs are?
- Am I a deliberate husband, or do I just take life as it comes each day?
- Does she know that I am committed to her and to our marriage no matter what?

In the Ephesians passages we looked at earlier in this chapter, we notice that Jesus not only gave himself up for his bride, but he also came to "sanctify her, cleansing her by the washing of water with the word, that He might present to Himself the church in all her glory, having no spot or wrinkle or any such thing; … "

Christ not only came to redeem us (his bride) and bring us into a personal relationship with himself, but he also came to *sanctify* us. The word sanctify is typically translated "holy" or "blameless." The Greek word is *hagiazo*, and it carries with it the idea of being separated out from among something for a special purpose. God has called you and me to be separated from this world unto himself so that we might reflect his love and demonstrate to this world that he is our Father God and bring him glory in the process. The word for *spot* is literally "no impurity," and *wrinkle* means "no sign of age."

When Paul uses this analogy with Christ sanctifying his church, he shows husbands that part of their role is to be a servant in a way that helps their wives become godly women by encouraging them in their walks with Jesus. We are to protect our wives from anything in our lives that is impure, evil, or harmful, as well as help shoulder those life burdens that weigh them down and make them age and feel older than they really are.

Servant husbands must be willing and able to be the spiritual leaders in their marriages and not relinquish that role to their wives. This doesn't mean we can't delegate aspects of this role, but ultimately, we as husbands will stand before God and answer to him as to whether or not we acted as the spiritual heads of our marriages and our homes.

There's nothing more frustrating for a wife than to think she has to be the spiritual leader in the family because her husband isn't willing to do so. We must willingly take whatever action is necessary to serve in this capacity, realizing that this is our God-given responsibility and privilege. This is our primary ministry—above teaching, witnessing, or leading Bible studies and small groups. Only our personal, daily walk with him should take precedence.

This is why Paul wrote in Ephesians 2:10, "For we are God's workmanship, created in Christ Jesus to do good works, which God prepared in advance for us to do."

The husband's primary "good work" is to be a servant-leader and to encourage his wife to love and do good works.

R.C. Sproul makes this observation:
"Would a woman be afraid to submit herself to a man who loved her as much as Jesus loved the church?"

Here's another example of what this kind of love looks like:

Robertson McQuilkin was the president of Colombia Bible College and Seminary. In 1990, he announced his resignation as president, because of his wife Muriel, who was suffering from advanced Alzheimer's disease. This was part of his resignation letter:

> *My dear wife, Muriel, has been in failing mental health for about eight years. So far I have been able to carry both her ever-growing needs and my leadership responsibilities at Columbia Bible College. But recently it has become apparent that Muriel is contented most of the time she is with me and almost none of the time when I am away from her. It is not just "discontent." She is filled with fear—even terror—that she has lost me and always goes in search of me when I leave home. Then she may be full of anger when she cannot get to me. So it is clear to me that she needs me now, full-time.... The decision was made, in a way, 42 years ago when I promised to care for Muriel "in sickness and in health.... till death do us part."... As a man of my word, integrity has something to do with it. But so does fairness. She has cared for me fully and sacrificially all these years; if I cared for her for the next 40 years I would not be out of debt. Duty, however, can be grim and stoic. But there is more; I love Muriel. She is a delight to me—her childlike dependence and confidence in me, her warm love, and occasional flashes of that wit I used to relish so, her happy spirit and tough resilience in the face of her continual distressing frustration. I do not have to care for her, I get to! It is a high honor to care for so wonderful a person. (Disciplines of a Godly Man, Hughes, pp. 33–34)*

> In this same way, husbands ought to *love their wives* **as their own bodies**. He who loves his wife loves himself. After all, no one ever hated his own body, but he feeds and cares for it, just as Christ does the church — for we are members of his body. "For this reason a man will leave his father and mother and be united to his wife, and the two will become one flesh." This is a profound mystery—but I am talking about Christ and the church. *Ephesians 5:28-32*

Everyone naturally wants to take care of his or her own body. We feed our bodies, we clothe them, we protect them from cold and heat and generally help them grow and stay healthy. Paul is simply stating the obvious that just as a husband spends a lifetime taking care of his own body, so a husband ought to love his wife as his own body, nurturing, protecting, feeding, clothing, and generally helping his wife grow in all aspects, including the spiritual. In fact, Paul thinks it absurd for a husband to do anything less if he truly loves and desires to be a servant to his wife.

"... he feeds and cares for it, just as Christ does the church ..."
Again, Paul shows how Christ loves his body—the body of Christ—and would never do anything to hurt her or keep her from growing and maturing. He gave himself up for her and has served her in a way to redeem her and bring her back into an eternal relationship. And Paul wants our relationships with our wives to be similar, as we nurture, love, and serve them.

The word *feed* (or *nourish*) is a bird metaphor that means "to feed to maturity." *Care for* (or *cherish*) is another bird metaphor meaning "to warm." These two terms should motivate every mature Christian husband's actions toward his wife. Husbands are stewards of their wives' (and children's) gifts, as well as their own!

"For this reason a man will leave his father and mother and be united to his wife, and the two will become one flesh" *Genesis 2:24*.

A marriage relationship severs one type of relationship and forms an entirely new relationship. When a son leaves his father and mother, he leaves the parent-child relationship to create a new union with a woman, with the ultimate goal of becoming one flesh.

This type of intimate relationship is reserved only for that couple. It is a relationship that is meant to be unbreakable. Marriage is also a reflection of the relationship Christ has with us and what it cost him. Christ will never forsake us, and we must never forsake our wife and our marriage.

The intent of Paul's thought here is not to delve into the matter of divorce, but he certainly implies how a healthy God-centered relationship works and how that relationship flourishes after the pattern of Christ being the head and bridegroom of the church.
This is why he says in Ephesians 5:32-33, "This is a profound mystery—but I am talking about Christ and the church. However, each one of you also must love his wife as he loves himself, and the wife must respect her husband."

Paul says that as the true bride of Christ, we can be assured that our bridegroom will bring us home to be with himself, because we are united to him in a spiritual union that God brought together and no man can separate.

This is a great mystery and also an amazing blessing to know that our Lord and Savior loved us enough to die a gruesome death on a cross and take the punishment for our sins. He made the first move. He didn't wait for us to get right, to get our acts together, or to even clean up our lives before he acted on our behalf. He did all of that because he loved us.

Some husbands think it is a sign of weakness to even think about submitting to the desires or needs of their wives. Others are just so stubborn that they feel their wives must take the first step before they will budge. Their relationships with their wives don't resemble the relationship between Christ and his bride at all.

Instead of "*loving her as Christ loves*," they stubbornly refuse to be the first to love or submit, and they wait for their wives to always take the first step.

In your subconscious, it may sound like, "I'll love her when she begins to submit" or "I'll help her out more when she quits nagging me about working too late or spending time with my friends." This kind of love sounds pretty conditional, doesn't it?

Paul also mentions the mystery of this relationship we have with Christ in his letter to the Romans: "But God demonstrates his own love for us in this: While we were still sinners, Christ died for us" *Romans 5:8.*

I am not to wait for my wife to become a better person before I start loving and serving her. My care and love for her is not dependent upon her actions. My leadership and submission to her does not take into account conditions or provisions. And remember, this is *not* a suggestion from God!

Even as Christ loved us while we were still sinners, we must love our wives regardless of their performance. As we commit (with God's help) to love her unconditionally and seek his will and agenda for our marriages, our homes will become a picture of the relationship Christ has with his bride.

In doing this, Christ is glorified.

So as not to forget what our roles are in marriage, Paul repeats it one more time in Ephesians 5:33: "However, each one of you also *must love his wife* as he loves himself, and the wife must respect her husband."
In this one simple verse, God tells us a *huge* key to a happy married life: The primary need of your wife is to *feel* loved by you. That feeling comes in many forms, but she needs to experience your attention, your validation of her, your respect for her, your praise and admiration, your sincere interest in the things she feels are important, and your continued physical and verbal affection.

This is the summary statement of the entire passage. The husband is commanded to continue to love his wife as himself, and the wife is called on to yield to and respect her husband. This is truly a bottom line verse for marriage relationships.

Colossians 3:19

Husbands, love your wives and do not be harsh with them.

Ask Christian husbands to summarize their biblical duty in one word, and most will likely answer leadership. But God answers the question with a different word: love.

There is no doubt that if you're a husband, God's design for you includes the aspect of leadership. But it is a leadership that flows from love and is always tempered by tender, caring affection. The husband's proper role as a loving, nurturing head is best epitomized by Christ, who took the servant's role to serve and love his bride.

"Husbands, love your wives …"

In Matthew 19, when Jesus's disciples heard him teach on the permanence of marriage and the sinfulness of divorce, they exclaimed, "If this is the situation between a husband and wife, it is better not to marry!" But here, Paul ups the ante—not only must a man live with his wife for the rest of his life, he must actively, purposefully love his wife for the rest of his life.

The Greek word used here for love is *agapao*. It is a present tense imperative indicating continuous action. The verb is used to express a willing love, not the love of passion or emotion but the love of choice, a covenant kind of love. It could be translated "keep on loving no matter what."

According to the Bible, love is something you *do*, so we could conclude that how much you love is determined by how much you do. Therefore, we should say "I love you" to our wife primarily by our actions.

"… do not be harsh with them."

harsh = Greek to make bitter, provoke, irritate

The Greek word for embittered is translated *pikraino*, which originally meant pointed and sharp. In reference to the senses, it is "like a pervasive smell, a shrill noise, a painful feeling." It also means "to have bitter resentment or even hatred toward someone." Bitterness refers to what is caustic, resentful, or sarcastic; the recipient of another's bitter words or actions; or experiencing an emotion that is distasteful or distressing.

We shouldn't display harshness of temper or resentment toward our wives. We are not to irritate or exasperate them, but rather we are to provide loving leadership in the home. Remember, as husbands we are called to seek how we may please our wives.

As we discovered earlier, a husband must love his wife with tender and faithful affection, as Christ loved the church and as he loves his own body. In addition, he must not be bitter toward her and not treat her unkindly with harsh language or severe treatment but instead be kind and obliging to her in all things.

God designed a wife to be submissive within a context of love. In that way, she is protected, because a man who truly loves his wife would never force her to submit to something that is abusive, humiliating, degrading, or in violation of her conscience.

If he is angry about something his wife said or did, a man can have the tendency to become hard or overbearing. Only Christ's love can counter this inclination to harshness.

Language that is caustic, bitter, resentful, or sarcastic is especially hurtful to women. Women receive and respond to words differently than men. You can be sharp or sarcastic with a guy friend, and he will shrug it off or even laugh about it. But if you do that with your wife, you will wound her deeply, far more than you may realize. So, with God's help, put off these tendencies toward criticism and sarcasm.

Your love for her will demonstrate the great and profound mystery of the union of Christ with his people as you tenderly nourish and cherish her, showering upon her the grace and love that God has showered upon you. And as you give yourself to her, you will find the strength to bear with her even when she's being unreasonable and the ability to be patient - even when she's being unlovable. This is love. (See 1 Corinthians 13.)

> **It is this love that God calls you to.**
> **It is this love that you are to bestow upon your wife.**
> **Not because she deserves it, but because Christ deserves it.**

I Peter 3: 7

> **Husbands, in the same way be considerate as you live with your wives, and treat them with respect as the weaker partner and as heirs with you of the gracious gift of life, so that nothing will hinder your prayers.**

Peter is speaking of being considerate. Other translations use the word *understanding*. This virtue is incompatible with the kind of independent, proud, self-absorbed macho mystique many seem to think epitomizes true maleness today. It calls for understanding, sensitivity, and the ability to meet your wife's needs. It involves a sincere effort to understand her desires, feelings, fears, concerns, anxieties, goals, and dreams.

Mainly, it boils down to knowing her. We need to become students of our wives. We need to read about marriage, wives and how to better understand them. We need to deliberately and actively listen to them and ask God to help us better understand our wives' hearts.

How can you express a sacrificial love that is considerate of her needs when you have no earthly idea what her needs are? There are many books available today dedicated to identifying what those needs are and how we can meet them. In general, the most identified needs of a wife are usually found in these categories:

> ## A wife needs …
>
> *1. A husband who is committed to her and their marriage no matter what.*
>
> *2. A husband who is walking with Jesus and trying to lead her spiritually.*
>
> *3. A husband who praises her and makes her feel special.*
>
> *4. A husband who values and cherishes her.*
>
> *5. A husband who provides for her and makes her feel secure.*
>
> *6. A husband who protects her physically, emotionally, and spiritually.*
>
> *7. A husband who listens and allows her to process life.*
>
> *8. A husband who communicates with her and allows her into his world.*
>
> *9. A husband who invests in her life and invites her to flourish as a person.*
>
> *10. To know that she is meeting her husband's vital needs.*

Husbands are to continually grant wives their due respect (honor) and not take liberties with leadership "rights." Honor refers to the worth or merit of some object. It is the amount at which something is valued. A related word, *timios*, is translated "precious" in 1 Peter 1:19.

Wives are to be treasured as one would treasure a precious stone. Husbands are to show their wives that they are precious by spending time with them, talking with them, praying with them, protecting them, and loving them as Christ loved the church.

The wife is *"the weaker vessel,"* according to this verse. This has reference primarily to the physical realm. In general, women are physically weaker than men.

We are to serve our wives with our strength. We should treat them as the weaker vessel, showing them a particular deference in matters where their physical weakness places them at a disadvantage. This verse actually suggests that God designed women to be under the protection of men, benefiting from their strength. Serving our wives by lending them that strength is one of the main ways we show them a Christ-like, sacrificial love.

We're also to regard our wives *"as being heirs together of the grace of life."* Men and women may be unequal physically, but they are equal spiritually. We must treat our wives as spiritual equals. Your role as her leader does not mean you are her superior. Both of you are utterly dependent on divine grace and are heirs of that grace together.

The spirit-filled husband loves his wife, not for what she can do for him but because of what he can do for her. That is exactly how Christ's love works. He loves us not because there's something in us that attracts him, not because he gains any benefit from loving us, but simply because he determined to love us and delights to bestow his favor on us.

> I remember the story of a married couple who lived long enough to celebrate their fiftieth wedding anniversary. Although they had been married for fifty years, they behaved as if they were newlyweds. They were obviously very happy together. They obviously loved being together.
>
> At their anniversary celebration, a guest asked the husband, "What has been the key to maintaining your happiness in marriage through all these years?" Without a moment's hesitation, he replied, "It's simple, really. We are both madly in love with the same person. We are both madly in love with Jesus Christ."

Indeed, when a man and a woman both love the Lord Jesus with all their hearts, souls, minds, and strength, they can expect to find a happy marriage.

Chrysostom (Archbishop of Constantinople) gave husbands this timeless advice 1600 years ago:

A husband must never exercise his authority by insulting and abusing his wife.
Whenever you give your wife advice, always begin by telling her how much you love her.
Nothing will persuade her so well to admit the wisdom of your words as her assurance that you are speaking to her with sincere affection.

Show her that you value her company, and prefer being at home to being out.
Esteem her in the presence of your friends and children.
Praise and show admiration for her good acts.
And if she ever does anything foolish, advise her patiently.
Finally, never call her by her name alone, but with terms of endearment, honor, and love.
If you honor her, she won't need honor from others; she won't desire praise from others if she enjoys the praise that comes from you.
Prefer her before all others, both for her beauty and her discernment, and praise her.

"So that nothing will hinder your prayers."

The word *hindered* literally means "to cut from and so to interrupt." It was used as a military metaphor meaning to cut in on, throw obstacles in the way of, or cut up the road so that normal movement was impossible. It means to cause to cease by removing, to do away with, to eliminate and more figuratively, as in the present verse, to hinder, frustrate, impede, or retard.

The idea is that failure to treat your wife with understanding will get in the way and hamper a husband's attempts to pray. Your prayers to God will be "done away with," "frustrated," and "impeded."

Failure to give due honor to our wives will result in a cutting in on the effectiveness of prayer, both your individual prayers and your united prayer times.

Mark it down: A husband's domestic relationship to his wife has a profound impact on his spiritual fellowship with God. A husband's spiritual fellowship with God has a profound impact on his domestic relationship with his wife.

No Christian husband should presume to think that any spiritual good will be accomplished in his life without an effective ministry of prayer. And no husband may expect an effective prayer life unless he lives with his wife "*in an understanding way, granting her honor.*"

The point of this passage is simply this: our godly care and respect for our wives will keep a channel open to the throne of God. The result of treating our wives as God instructs is a beautiful, continual fellowship with God himself. This should be motivation enough for all husbands.

The Bottom Line

1. God has very specific requirements for husbands.

2. We are to love our wives as Christ loves the church.

3. Wives will respond to our loving, servant leadership.

4. If we know what is the right thing to do and don't do it, we are deliberately turning our backs on God and choosing self-focused independence (sin) and its consequences.

5. We need to become perpetual students of our wives and of their needs, desires, hopes, and fears.

> *When you marry someone you set them apart (sanctify them) from the world. They are set apart for special protection, special care, for special attention, for a special purpose.*

Part 3

God's Word—About Relationships

As the creator of husbands and wives, God knows better than anyone what each partner in a marriage needs in order to flourish.

In addition to his commandments for us as husbands, there are many scriptures that relate to our relationship with our wife but do not specifically address marriage. The following New Testament verses regarding relationships also greatly apply to life at home, and as such, should be taken as God's divine wisdom, exhortation, and expectation for us.

Romans 12:10 *Be devoted to one another in brotherly love. Honor one another above yourselves.*

Devoted is a great word. It means loyal, loving, or affectionate. As your closest relationship, does your wife know how devoted you are to her and to your marriage? Would she tell her friends that you are a loving and affectionate husband (not just when you want sex)? And did you catch the next sentence?

Honor one another *above yourself*. Wow. That's pretty impossible, huh? But since God says so, we had better choose to honor her above ourselves. Does that mean we are to always do what she says? No. But, we are to ask her opinion and advice, and consider it carefully when making decisions. We are also to honor her needs above our own. Do we know what those needs are, and how we can meet them? Maybe we should take the time to get with her, and ask.

1 Corinthians 13:4-6 *Love is patient, love is kind. It does not envy, it does not boast, it is not proud. It is not rude, nor self-seeking. It is not easily angered. It keeps no record of wrongs. Love does not delight in evil but rejoices in the truth.*

If you replaced your name for the word "love" in this passage, how would you measure up? If you fall way short, it is time to seriously ask God to make some changes in your heart, and help you to love her this way (as Christ loved the church).

Ephesians 4:29 *Do not let any unwholesome talk come out of your mouths, but only what is helpful for building others up according to their needs, that it may benefit those who listen.*

It doesn't say to say whatever pops into your mind, and then ask forgiveness later. It doesn't say you are justified by lashing out at her because she "deserved it". Words hurt. Words can also heal. We are being cautioned to watch what we say, and how we say it. Many times it is our tone, or facial expression that she will remember far longer than the words themselves. God wants us to think before we speak, and catch those hurtful, sarcastic, angry words before they leave our lips and cause severe damage. See Psalm 141:3.

> *Words kill, words give life; they're either poison or fruit—you choose.*
> *~Proverbs 18:21*

Ephesians 4:32 *Be kind and compassionate to one another, forgiving one another, just as Christ forgave you.*

Very simple. Are you kind and compassionate with your wife? Sometimes? Seldom? If not, you are not doing what God asks of you. We are called to treat her with the same measure of grace that He has treated (and still treats) us. And then we are told to forgive JUST AS Christ has forgiven us. We know He has forgiven us completely, and without any conditions. Are you holding anything against your wife? Have you completely forgiven her for things she may have said or done that hurt, offended or disappointed you? If you are, it's time to stop and deal with those, so you can move ahead in your relationship with a clean slate and a fresh start....and because we are told to do so.

Philippians 2:3-5 *Do nothing out of selfish ambition or vain conceit, but in humility consider others better than yourselves. Each of you should look not only to your own interests, but also to the interests of others. Your attitude should be the same as that of Christ Jesus.*

Do NOTHING out of selfish ambition, is impossible without some divine intervention. Only with His help can we even come close. Once again we are told to consider our wife better than ourself (I didn't say it – He did), and to look out for her interests along with our own. This is basically a call to humility. Our attitude is what He is calling us to keep in check. In order to have the same attitude as Christ Jesus, we must be willing to humble ourselves, take up our own cross, and follow His leadership (what He says) each and every day. Remember – God opposes the proud, but gives grace to the humble (I Peter 5:5, James 4:6)) – and you sure don't want God to be opposing you.

Colossians 3:12-13 *"Therefore, as God's chosen people, holy and dearly loved, clothe yourselves with compassion, kindness, humility, gentleness and patience. Bear with each other and forgive whatever grievances you may have against one another. Forgive as the Lord forgave you."*

Once again we are told, as God's people, that we should have these qualities in our life. They should especially be evident in our home. Do they come naturally to us? Probably not, but we are still told to "clothe" ourselves with them. This speaks of choosing to perform an action. We choose to clothe ourselves in real clothes every day, so we can also choose to put on these clothes as well. Again, it comes down to whether or not we will choose to.

There is that phrase again. We are told to forgive AS the Lord forgave….. completely, unconditionally.

1 Peter 3:8-9 *"Finally, all of you, live in harmony with one another; be sympathetic, love as brothers, be compassionate and humble. Do not repay evil for evil or insult for insult, but with blessing, because to this you were called so that you may inherit a blessing."*

All of us…. are to live in harmony with one another. How much more does this apply at home? Is there harmony in your home? Are you doing everything in your power, and calling on God for His, to create harmony with your wife? Are you being sympathetic to her needs, hurts, concerns and cares? Would she say you are being compassionate? And there is that word again – "humble". Dang it. We keep getting that one. Sooner or later we had just better get it through our thick heads, that humility is one huge key to enjoying a dynamic walk with God, and a fulfilling walk with our wife.

1 John 3:18 *"Dear children, let us not love with words or tongue, but with actions and in truth."*

Words are so easy. We said wonderful, loving things to our wives at our wedding ceremony. Here is the vow a husband promised in a recent wedding I had the honor of performing:

> *In the name of Jesus, I, ____, take you _____,*
> *to be my wife; to have and to hold from this day forward,*
> *for better or for worse, for richer, for poorer,*
> *in sickness and in health, to love and to cherish,*
> *until we are parted by death.*
> **This is my solemn vow.**

You most likely said something very similar to your young starry-eyed bride. God calls us to show this love and devotion by our actions and not just by our words. How have you done showing her (and God) how special she is to you? Have you lived up to your solemn vow?

We are commanded by God to love our wife as Christ loved us, and to give ourself up for her. This does not happen automatically. We must make conscious choices every day to actively and deliberately demonstrate that love to her, and to the world around us.

"We Need to Talk"

For a man, these may be the four most dreaded words in the English language, or any language for that matter.

If you research the Top 10 reasons couples get divorced, one of the leading causes seems to always be listed as a lack of communication or a breakdown in communication.

Communication: Men deplore it. Women crave it. Women run toward it. Men avoid it like the plague.

Why is it so hard for us guys? Why would we rather have a root canal or colonoscopy?

In her book, You Just Don't Understand: Women and Men in Conversation, sociolinguist Deborah Tannen shows that the differences between the communication styles of men and women go far beyond mere socialization, and appear to be inherent in the basic make up of each sex. Tannen observed that, "For males, conversation is the way you negotiate your status in the group and keep people from pushing you around; you use talk to preserve your independence. Females, on the other hand, use conversation to negotiate closeness and intimacy; talk is the essence of intimacy, so being best friends means sitting and talking. For boys, activities, doing things together, are central. Just sitting and talking is not an essential part of friendship. They're friends with the boys they do things with."

Tannen makes the point that both sexes need to understand the inherent differences in their communication styles so that they don't expect the impossible. There is middle ground where men and women can meet and find understanding. Women must learn that the kind of intimate talk they have with their girlfriends should remain just that. Trying to turn your man into a girlfriend will usually fail because men, in general, don't create feelings of closeness in that way. Men, too can understand that when their woman is talking, she is attempting to connect to him--she's not just talking to talk, nor is she trying to readjust the status of their relationship. By sharing more of himself he shows her, in a way she can understand, that he's not pushing her away; that he does indeed love her and want to be close to her.

We Are Indeed Created Differently

None of us needs an example (we have plenty of our own) – but here's one to ponder:

> Two women meet and one notices her friend's new hairstyle.
> "Wow, Jackie, did you get your hair cut?"
> "Yes, I went to Chez Felix! It was amazing." She does a razor cut and twirl. "Don't you just love it?"
> Studying Jackie's hair as though searching for a lost set of car keys, Jackie's friend takes in a deep breath. "It's absolutely to die for! It's so much better than how your other girl cut it. And the style! I can't believe how thin it makes you look."
> Jackie wrinkles her face. "You're sure it doesn't make my neck look too long?"
> "Too long?" Her friend gasps. "Definitely not. You look like a model. I love the way it curls under, and it's so shiny."
> It could go on that way for a long time, and neither woman would get bored with the topic. Take a man in the same situation. If he notices that his friend got a haircut (which is a huge assumption to begin with), he might say something like, "Hey, got your ears lowered, huh?"
> To which his friend will say something profound like, "Yep."
> Conversation over.

Gary Smalley, who has written extensively about marriage, says that a woman requires ten thousand words a day to communicate. But a man needs only two thousand words each day. So, don't be surprised when you come home exhausted from work and are finished talking for the day and discover that she is just getting started. This is especially true if she has been at home with the kids all day and has had little, if any, adult conversation.

<u>Men are intellectual processors</u>. We talk to express thoughts, solve problems, and arrive at conclusions. When talking about a problem, men instinctively want to get to the bottom line.

<u>A woman tends to be an emotional processor</u>. Your wife talks about her problem primarily to process her emotions, not her thoughts. She's not wasting words or time. Most of the time she doesn't even want to reach a conclusion or have you "fix" the problem.

<u>Men communicate to share information</u>. They are not necessarily looking to establish a relationship. We keep our information sharing to a minimum. We get to the point, state it, and are then usually done.

<u>Women communicate to establish relationships</u>. Because of this, they tend to be more talkative and more personal in their conversation. Women are interested in the how, the why, and the feelings and emotions of a situation.

Volumes have been written about the differences between men and women and what potential problems these characteristics can cause in a marriage, especially involving communication. Becoming a better communicator and a better listener are crucial for husbands as we seek to love and serve our wives, and I recommend we all become lifelong students of these essential marriage skills.

Many times, these communication differences and the frustrations they cause become convenient excuses, and we conclude "Oh well, we're just different." Although it may be true, we have a mandate from God to appreciate and work through our differences and strive to "live with her in an understanding way." (See I Peter 3:7)

Men, we must keep in mind that it was God who created these differences, and we need to seek him for wisdom to better understand them. This, too, is a deliberate, continual process and an integral part of oneness.

I am convinced that God made Adam a gardener before he brought him a wife so he could learn to nurture and care for God's gift to him. He knew very well that a beautiful garden was the result of much deliberate attention and loving care. He learned very quickly that he needed to "tend" to his wife in a very similar fashion.

Words Matter...

God created man to be the head of the home, and it is up to us to set the mood and the emotion in our homes. If things are stressful, tense, irritable, or even hostile at home, we need to take a good inventory of our own hearts before God. We are going to be held accountable one day.

Some of you remember the old rhyme "sticks and stone may break my bones, but words can never hurt me." As kids, we used to recite this whenever someone said something very hurtful about us or to us. It made us feel somewhat better at the time, but the truth is that those words still hurt!

Words are powerful. Words count.

> **Words kill, words give life; they're either poison or fruit—you choose.**
> **Proverbs 18:21 (MSG)**

The words you speak to your wife can either bring her life or death, can either build her up or tear her down, can bring encouragement or discouragement—you get the idea.

Based on the verses we have already discussed, are you using words that covey:

Christ-like love (Ephesians 5)
Harshness (Colossians 3)
Consideration (1 Peter 3) or
Respect (1 Peter 3)?

In addition to these, God gives us many instructions about the words we speak and the way we say them, especially to our wives.

- **Psalm 19:14** "May the words of my mouth and the meditation of my heart be pleasing in your sight, O Lord, my Rock and my Redeemer."
- **Proverbs 10:11** "The mouth of the righteous is a fountain of life."
- **Proverbs 10:19** "When words are many, sin is not absent, but he who holds his tongue is wise."
- **Proverbs 12:14** "From the fruit of his lips a man is filled with good things as surely as the work of his hands rewards him."
- **Proverbs 12:18** "Reckless words pierce like a sword, but the tongue of the wise brings healing."
- **Proverbs 13:3** "He who guards his lips guards his life, but he who speaks rashly will come to ruin."
- **Proverbs 15:1** "A gentle answer turns away wrath, but a harsh word stirs up anger."
- **Proverbs 15:4** "The tongue that brings healing is a tree of life, but a deceitful tongue crushes the spirit."
- **Proverbs 16:24** "Pleasant words are a honeycomb, sweet to the soul and healing to the bones."
- **Proverbs 17:14** "Starting a quarrel is like breaching a dam; so drop the matter before a dispute breaks out."
- **Proverbs 17:19** "He who loves a quarrel loves sin; he who builds a high gate invites destruction."
- **Proverbs 17:27** "A man of knowledge uses words with restraint, and a man of understanding is even-tempered."
- **Proverbs 18:13** "He who answers before listening—that is his folly and his shame."
- **Proverbs 21:23** "He who guards his mouth and his tongue keeps himself from calamity."
- **Proverbs 26:21** "As charcoal to embers and as wood to fire, so is a quarrelsome man for kindling strife."

- **Ecclesiastes 10:12** "Words from a wise man's mouth are gracious."
- **Matthew 7:12** "So in everything, do to others what you would have them do to you."
- **Matthew 12:36** "Men will have to give account on the day of judgment for every careless word they have spoken."

- **James 3: 5-10** "Likewise the tongue is a small part of the body, but it makes great boasts. Consider what a great forest is set on fire by a small spark. The tongue also is a fire, a world of evil among the parts of the body. It corrupts the whole person, sets the whole course of his life on fire, and is itself set on fire by hell. "All kinds of animals, birds, reptiles and creatures of the sea are being tamed and have been tamed by man, but no man can tame the tongue. It is a restless evil, full of deadly poison. With the tongue we praise our Lord and Father, and with it we curse men, who have been made in God's likeness. Out of the same mouth come praise and cursing."

- **1 Peter 3: 8-12** "Finally, all of you, live in harmony with one another; be sympathetic, love as brothers, be compassionate and humble. Do not repay evil with evil or insult with insult, but with blessing, because to this you were called so that you may inherit a blessing. For, "Whoever would love life and see good days must keep his tongue from evil and his lips from deceitful speech.""

God devotes many verses in his word to our words, our tongues, and how we are to speak with each other. As the leaders of our homes, men are responsible to lead by example in the words we choose, the tone we use in conversation, and the overall mood of our home.

Do you use harsh, biting words with your wife and children? Are you tempted to throw darts at your spouse as sarcastic payback for words she has launched at you? Is your choice of words meant to build up your wife or tear her down? Are you being respectful in your choice of words and the tone of your voice? God takes words seriously, and so should we. We can each recall words spoken to us by a class bully, a fickle girlfriend, or an errant coach who thought their words would motivate us to perform but actually tore us down.

How much more do our words cut our wives (and children) to the bone when spoken in anger, jest, or retaliation? Men more easily forget. We jest with each other, tease each other, and think it's funny.

Wives don't find it funny at all. *And* they don't forget.

Pause

Let's hit the pause button for a minute here. The Scriptures we just read are straight from God's heart.

If you're like me, it is easy to just read over them and get on with the task at hand—finishing the book.

God's word to us was not written with the intention of being read like a novel for entertainment or to make us feel spiritual. His words to us are not meant to be stored on a bedside table or used to fill a gap on a bookshelf. His words are *living* and *active*, and he continues to speak to us each and every time we read them. The Bible is the only book ever written that comes with the author.

I encourage you to start a habit of approaching scripture as a conversation starter with God. Because these are not just words on a page but a direct message to us as his children, the Bible is important to our lives and to the discovery of the abundant, amazing life he promises.

Go back to the previous list of verses about our words and tongues. Read one verse and then stop and ask God to show you how you are doing when it comes to communicating with your wife. What does he want to say to *you* in each verse? Listen to what he says. If you don't hear anything, ask again. Repeat this process for each verse.

Is there something you need to ask him to forgive you for (words, anger, pride)? What about your wife? Is he asking you to humble yourself and apologize to her for something you said or the biting, cynical tone you used? Are you using silence or retreating (a common man tactic) as a weapon against your wife? Ask him to help you respond to and talk with your family in a loving and respectful manner.

God continually speaks to us. Will we take the time to listen?

> King David gave us a model for meeting with God: "Let the morning bring me word of your unfailing love, for I have put my trust in you. Show me the way I should go, for to you I lift up my soul" (Ps. 143:8). "My sheep hear My voice, and I know them, and they follow Me" *John 10:27.*
>
> "Behold, I stand at the door and knock, if anyone hears my voice and opens the door, I will come in to them and will dine with them, and he with Me" *Revelation 3:20.*

We are created to commune and communicate with God.... Try it.

The Bottom Line

1. We wield the power of life and death with our words.

2. God takes words seriously and will hold us accountable for ours.

3. God commands us to love, respect, and bless our wives in word and deed.

4. We set the tone and atmosphere in our homes by our words.

5. Words matter, especially to our wives.

6. God will speak to us and lead us if we will listen and allow him.

Words—so innocent and powerless as they are,
as standing in a dictionary, how potent for good
and evil they become in the hands of one
who knows how to combine them!
~ Nathaniel Hawthorne

Kind words may be short ...
but their echoes are endless.
~ Mother Theresa

No Way, Jose´

Let's face it, by now you are thinking, "No way. I can't do all that" or "I will never measure up."

You're telling me that all I have to do is……..Love my wife as Christ loves his church, Become less "me" focused and more "her" focused, Obey all of God's word concerning my relationship with my wife, Watch out for every word I speak, and Meet all of her needs.

No way! What's the use? That's an impossible list. I'm bound to fail.

As weird as it may seem, that is a great place to get to. That is exactly where God wants you.

"No matter what our situation in life—our deepest and most pressing need is to learn to walk with God. To hear His voice, to follow Him intimately. It brings us back to the source of life." ~ John Eldredge, Walking with God

There is no way a man, even a sincere, well-meaning, Christian man, can ever follow all the rules and consistently do all the right things—no matter how well-meaning or good-hearted he is. We are all in the same boat. Our best just isn't good enough and never will be.

"You can't possibly master enough principles and disciplines to ensure that your life works out. You weren't meant to and God won't let you."
~ John Eldredge, Walking with God

I am so thankful for Jesus's example.

He left his throne in heaven and "took upon himself the form of a man," and "humbled himself." (Phil 2:8) He left his God-likeness in heaven and became 100 percent human so he could show us how to live our lives well. If he would have lived as some sort of super hero, with godlike powers, then we could have never followed his example. It would have been impossible.

Listen to what he says about himself:

> **Matthew 26:39** "And He went a little beyond them, and fell on His face and prayed, saying, 'My Father, if it is possible, let this cup pass from Me; yet not as I will, but as You will.'"
>
> **John 5:19** "Therefore Jesus answered and was saying to them, 'Truly, truly, I say to you, the Son can do nothing of Himself, unless it is something He sees the Father doing; for whatever the Father does, these things the Son also does in like manner.'"
>
> **John 5:30** "I can do nothing on My own initiative As I hear, I judge; and My judgment is just, because I do not seek My own will, but the will of Him who sent Me."
>
> **John 8:28** "So Jesus said, 'When you lift up the Son of Man, then you will know that I am He, and I do nothing on My own initiative, but I speak these things as the Father taught Me.'"
>
> **John 12:49** "For I did not speak on My own initiative, but the Father Himself who sent Me has given Me a commandment as to what to say and what to speak."
>
> **John 14:10** "Do you not believe that I am in the Father, and the Father is in Me? The words that I say to you I do not speak on My own initiative, but the Father abiding in Me does His works."

As hard as it is for our minds to grasp, Jesus could not do anything on his own. He had no special powers, abilities, or gifts. He had no special training or pedigree. He was like me and you—desperate for God to work in and through him. Jesus' very words tell us that he only did what he saw and heard the Father doing. He only spoke what he heard the Father saying.

So, how are we to be good husbands? How are we to be good fathers, bosses, employees, citizens, or anything else?

> *"I am the vine, you are the branches; he who abides in Me and I in him, he bears much fruit, for apart from Me you can do nothing."*
> ~ John 15:5

The honest answer is that we have to learn to abide in the vine (Jesus) in order for there to be any fruit (results) in our personal and married lives. Abiding doesn't just happen. It isn't an automatic by-product of becoming a Christian, going to church, or even reading the Bible. Jesus may be our Savior, but we have to choose for him to be our Lord. This is a daily, moment-by-moment decision.

Another example Jesus uses in the book of John is that of a shepherd and his sheep. Jesus is the perfect, loving, lay-down-his-life-for-his-sheep shepherd, and—you guessed it—we are his sheep. Sheep are completely dependent on their shepherd.

How Do We Actually Do This?

In the example of the vine, we are told to abide in Christ. The word *abide* basically means to "dwell" or "live." We must learn to dwell and live our days "with" or "in" Christ. We need to cultivate a relationship with Christ similar to that which Jesus had with His Father—desperate, listening, watching, seeking, humbled—knowing full well that we can produce no good thing on our own. In the example of the shepherd, we are called Christ's sheep. Are we choosing to stay close to the shepherd, listen to his voice, and do what he says? Or are we running off through the pasture, living life on our own terms, our own way, and only coming near to him when we get hurt or want our needs met?

What would life be like if we developed a lifestyle of staying close to Jesus, listening to his voice, and eagerly doing what he asks of us? Would living in his presence and completely trusting him to lead and bless us change the way we approach our days, our weeks, our plans, our very lives?

When Jesus was asked what it took to follow him, he replied, "If any man will come after me, let him deny himself, take up his cross daily, and follow me" Luke 9:23.

The Bottom Line

The bottom line as Jesus saw it is this:

1. *Deny yourself.* Realize that you are totally incapable of doing this alone and realize that you are in desperate need for Jesus to speak to you, empower you, and lead your life.

2. *Take up your cross daily.* Make choices throughout the day to die to your self-focused life/agenda and willingly submit to his.

3. *Follow me.* By definition, following implies that someone else is leading. At any point during your day/week/month/life, you are either leading or allowing Jesus to lead. There is no neutral ground. You either have your face or back to him.

That, my brothers, is the Christian life in a nutshell. That is the bottom line to living in victory in your marriage and in your life.

Most of us have already heard this before, but sadly, very few of us actually *do* it. We have knowledge of it. We mentally agree with it. But we don't practice it.

We are not unlike the Pharisees in Jesus' day. Here is what Jesus said to them:

> **You study the Scriptures carefully. You study them because you think they will give you eternal life. The Scriptures you study give witness about me. But you refuse to come to me and receive life. John 5:39-40**

Jesus didn't come to earth so we could know *about* him. He came so we could really *know* him. He wants us to really know him—as a person—with emotions, feelings, plans, desires, etc.

> **I will give them a heart to know Me, for I am the Lord; and they will be My people, and I will be their God. Jeremiah 24:7**

> **I am the good shepherd, and I know My own and My own know Me. John 10:14**

Knowing God is not only possible, it is what we are created for. The very first person Adam and Eve laid eyes upon was God himself. God longs for us to know him.

> Here I am! I stand at the door and knock. If anyone hears my voice and opens the door, I will come in and eat with him, and he with me. *Revelation 3:20*

For years I thought that this familiar verse in Revelation 3:20 was in reference to unsaved people asking Jesus to "come into their hearts" for the first time. Read in context, the verse is actually written to the lukewarm church at Laodicea—to people who already "know" him. He is asking them to willingly open the door of their hearts so he can walk with them and enjoy life together.

The main "illness" in the church at Laodicea was the same one that has reached epidemic proportions in the world today—apathy. We honestly don't want Jesus coming in and messing things up. We pretty much like things the way they are. We know we could probably do better or experience more, but it would probably require more work and effort, so we settle for being lukewarm.

During my personal research into marriage and how I could become a better mentor and advisor to married couples, I recently sat down with several pastors in my community to ask them what they saw as the biggest reason for discord in the relationships of married couples they counseled.

Was the issue based in communication, sexuality, child rearing, or finances?

Without exception, they all agreed that the **bottom line** issue facing the vast majority of couples in crisis was that neither spouse spends time reading the Bible or praying. They may have the occasional quiet time or read a quick devotional; they may attend church regularly and attend a small group meeting. However, they aren't seeking God or attempting to walk with him on a daily basis. They are not desperate to hear his voice and follow where he leads.

> *They desperately want the benefits of a Christian marriage, but they are unwilling to pay the price to enjoy one.*

That is so like our American culture today. We want the best of everything but don't want to "pay" for it. The deception is that we convince ourselves that we just don't have the time, and that makes us feel better—as if we've addressed the issue. The truth is that we all have time; we just don't want it bad enough. Men rise at three o'clock in the morning to drive to a bitterly cold duck blind or deer stand because they want to. We find time to watch six hours of football on a Sunday afternoon, go jogging for an hour every morning, and work in the yard all weekend.

We *do* have the time. We just lack the *want* to. Do you remember a time in your life when you really, really wanted something so bad that you sacrificed a lot to get it? Maybe it was grades, sports, a job, health, etc.

When I was in ninth grade, I was so skinny that I had to walk by a spot twice to cast a shadow. I wanted desperately to play football, and I knew the only way that would be even remotely possible was if I was physically bigger and stronger. I wanted it so much that I spent hours in the weight room. I even worked out at home with dumbbells. I ate food unfit for human consumption in order to take on more calories and protein. I paid the price, because I wanted it deeply. And it paid off. I grew bigger and stronger and went on to start for two years on our championship football team.

Jesus Was the Most Desperate Man in History

He knew that he could only do what the Father told him to do and say only what the Father told him to say. He prayed, he asked, he sought—he was desperate to hear. "And in the morning, rising up a great while before day, he went out, and departed into a solitary place, and there prayed" (Mark 1:35).

In spite of a grueling schedule and thousands of people demanding his time and attention, Jesus rose early to pray. He was tired. He'd had a busy day. Surely he deserved some rest, but he was desperate. He came "to do the Father's will, not his own." (John 6:38) So, he prayed. He talked with the Father, and the Father talked back. He told Jesus what to say, where to go, what to do, and what his will was for the moment, the day, the week. Notice what else Jesus did—he obeyed. He heard the Father speak, and he did what the Father said.

As helpful as they are, reading more books, hearing more sermons, and attending more seminars won't give you the life you long for. Jesus knew the scripture, he attended church, he walked with Christian friends, but he was still desperate for a moment-by-moment, intimate relationship with God himself.

Do you want to be fulfilled in life? Want to experience an amazing marriage? Want to know what the abundant life really means?

Then learn to walk (abide) with him, every day. Live with your face toward God, not your back. Draw near to him and enjoy the "fullness of joy" in his presence. We are all created to enjoy intimacy with God, and we will not experience life fully until we do.

> ***You will make known to me the path of life; In Your presence is fullness of joy; In Your right hand there are pleasures forever. ~ Psalms 16:11***

Part 4

How Do I Get There From Here? Part 1

How do you go from your current, lukewarm, part-time Christian walk – to an adventure-filled relationship that you can't wait to see unfold every day?

Well, how did I go from being single to being married? I met someone—someone who was like no one else I had ever met, someone who captivated my heart, my mind, and my emotions. This woman became the center of my life. I *wanted* to spend as much time with her as I could every day. I *wanted* to share my life with her, talk with her, and be around her. I *wanted* to feel her love and affection for me, and I couldn't wait to express mine for her.

My son Wes met such a girl in high school. He and his friends called her "the goddess," because she was "unapproachable." She was too beautiful, too popular, too everything for mere mortals to be around her.

He supposed she could never be attracted to him. What would his life be like if the goddess actually knew him and (miracle of miracles) actually liked him? My, how his life would change.

Sadly, many of us grow up in a world where we consciously, or subconsciously, think the same thing about God. He lives high on a mountain and is unapproachable by anyone except the spiritually "popular" or superior—surely not by the likes of sinful me. He probably knows who I am but is busy handling things for much more important people in the world.

We have fallen for the lie that tells us, we are not worthy of his time or attention, and surely not his affection.

My friend, the only way you will ever experience the joy and abundance of walking with God himself, as you were created to, is to begin to get to know him. Hear me out on this. I didn't say know *about* him; we must get to know the person of Jesus.

Wes knew a lot *about* the goddess. He knew where she went to school, where she lived, what she liked to do, who she hung around with, and where she was going to college. He even knew her laugh, her friends, her habits, and her ambitions. But he had never spent five minutes in her presence. He knew so much about her, but he wasn't involved and didn't have a relationship with her at all.

Isn't that the same with Jesus? We know what he said, what he did, who he hung out with, and what others said about him. We know about his family and friends and even about the amazing miracles he performed. We know details about his horrific death and are joyous to hear about his resurrection.

But do we really know him as a person? Have we spent much time in his company? Have we recognized his voice and felt his affection? Do we have a relationship with him, or are we content to know a lot about him and assume that we are Christ-followers? Remember the Pharisees. They were the "godliest" people of their day, but when Jesus walked among them, they did not recognize him or listen to him.

I contend that few Christians today have an intimate, personal, vibrant, daily relationship with Jesus himself. And that's why so many Christian couples struggle in their marriages.

A Personal Aside

For the vast majority of my Christian life (more than thirty-five years), I was one of those people. I knew much about Jesus but spent little time with him in a relationship. I naively thought that I was growing in my faith and maturing as a Christian man because I was learning more. I was acquiring more knowledge about Jesus and his Word, but I was lacking in a real, personal walk with the God of the universe. Spiritually, I was a mile wide and an inch deep.

I went to church every week, led youth meetings, and directed small group studies. I sang in the choir and even led worship. I tried to be a good husband and father and tried to live a good, moral life as best as I knew how. I tried to have a semi-consistent quiet time. But I was empty. I longed for more. Somewhere deep in my soul I knew there had to be more than that. Where was the life of the Christians I read about in Acts and throughout scripture? Where were the power, the joy, and the adventure? Something in my spirit was crying out for more. Like Peter, I wanted to get out of the boat and walk with Jesus!" Somehow, Peter knew that Jesus offered more than just sitting in the safety of the boat with his good Christian friends.

As I began to learn that a vibrant, exciting, moment-by-moment walk with Jesus was possible (and what he desires as well), I felt overwhelmed.

First, I realized that for years I believed the lie that I wasn't worthy. I thought that God was surely upset with me, even mad at me because of the life I had lived. I have sinned and fallen way short of what I should have done. I have let him and others down, and he must fold his arms in disgust with me.

That false belief led to the next conclusion—I thought that because God was mad at me, I must earn enough points to get back into his good graces. All of my Christian activity, as good as it was, was subconsciously carried out in hopes of earning enough *gold stars* for Jesus to accept me, or like me, or at least not punish me. I was performing—tap dancing for God.

I also became acutely aware that my poor relationship with my earthly father had a profound impact on how I viewed God, my heavenly Father. Very deep down in my soul I believed the lie that if my father could leave me, God might leave me too. If my dad could stop loving me, God could stop loving me. If I could never be good enough to please my dad, then God surely was impossible to please.

And so I stuffed all those feelings deep in the recesses of my heart. But God loved me too much to allow them to stay there. He began to reveal his love for me in profound and humbling ways. I was captivated with his love. I was overwhelmed with the reality of his affection for me. I began to experience chains falling off my life and freedom like I had never felt before.

God loves me! Yes, He loves the whole world, but He loves *me*! He *likes* me! He wants to hang out with me, walk with me, and enjoy my company. I am important to him. I matter to God! Wow!

My son Wes finally met the goddess. It was really nothing to write home about—he just met her socially, and they became acquainted. In high school, though, that is huge! *She knows who I am!* As a college freshman, he traveled to her university to visit mutual friends. They became reacquainted. He was enthralled once again, and they slowly became friends.

Well, as only God could do, Wes wrote us from school one day and announced that he was actually *dating* the goddess. Water turned to wine. Sick people healed. Seas parted. This was right up there in the realm of miracles.

He couldn't quit thinking about her. They talked on the phone until three and four in the morning. Then they woke up and called each other to talk some more. He was totally enthralled by love.

I, too, am now totally enthralled by love. The once unapproachable, distant, impersonal God is now the most captivating, loving, accepting, exciting person I have ever known. And the feeling is mutual! I am the apple of his eye. I am his beloved. I awake each morning, and He is there – knocking – asking me to open the door to my life, letting him come in and fellowship with me, guide me, counsel me, protect me, and just enjoy hanging out with me. He wants to be personally involved in the big things and the small things of my life. I am blown away! I don't want to miss another day of this adventure.

Getting Started

Unless we come to the personal realization that God, in Jesus, loves us, likes us, and wants to walk with us through every moment of every day, we will never get off the ground. We will have to wait until heaven to experience the exhilarating joy of knowing his love and walking in the profound joy of his presence.

The truth is this: the level of joy, intimacy, and fulfillment in our marriages will never rise above our personal intimacy with Christ. The creator of love—love himself—is the only one who can move in us to truly experience love and to be able to fully give it away to our wives.

We are all too familiar with the story in Genesis where Adam and Eve chose to live life on their own terms, ate the apple, and disobeyed God. Because of their sin, God writes:

> **So the Lord God banished him from the Garden of Eden to work the ground from which he had been taken. After he drove the man out, he placed on the east side of the Garden of Eden cherubim and a flaming sword flashing back and forth to guard the way to the tree of life. Genesis 3:23-24**

When man was banished from the Garden, he was also banished from the intimate, daily fellowship that Adam had enjoyed with his creator. When they chose to sin, Adam and Eve could no longer enjoy the sweet presence of their God as he walked and talked with them throughout their day.

I am honestly embarrassed to confess to you that what I am about to write was hidden from me for most of my Christian life. I write with the hope of passing on a profound truth that Jesus has revealed to me.

> Not only did God provide a way for mankind to escape the penalty of sin by having it paid for by the blood of the Lamb, Jesus, but that same sacrifice also paid the price for the sin that banished man from his presence. We can once again experience the moment-by-moment, intimate fellowship with the Father that he created us to enjoy in the Garden.
>
> The gate to the garden of God's presence has been reopened by Jesus. Sin no longer separates us from the continual loving presence of the Father. As believers, we have been forgiven our sins, past, present and future, and when God looks at us, he sees Jesus. He is in us, and we are in him.

John 14:20 "On that day you will realize that I am in my Father, and you are in me, and I am in you."

John 15:4 "Remain in me, and I will remain in you. No branch can bear fruit by itself; it must remain in the vine. Neither can you bear fruit unless you remain in me."

Psalms 16:11 "You have made known to me the path of life; you will fill me with joy in your presence, with eternal pleasures at your right hand."

Psalms 102:28 "The children of your servants will live in your presence."

Having paid the price for the sin that separated us from God in the first place, Jesus' death also offers us the amazing opportunity to again walk and talk with God in continual, daily fellowship. The gates to his presence are wide open, and he beckons us to draw near and enjoy the beautiful relationship we were created to enjoy.

Well, my son Wes married the goddess! He found God's handcrafted soul mate. Actually, God brought her to him in an amazing and wonderful way. He now enjoys a relationship that far exceeded his expectations only a few years ago.

In the same way, we can all enjoy a relationship with Jesus that we didn't think was possible either. God is so good.

Making Choices

Now that you know that an intimate, personal relationship with Jesus is not only possible but also sought after by him, the first decision you are faced with is this: will I choose to turn aside and move toward him?

We all know the story of Moses. Set adrift in the river by his mother, fetched by Pharaoh's daughter, and raised as royalty in Egypt. After killing an Egyptian soldier in anger, he fled to the desert to find solitude and refuge as a shepherd. God, however, had other plans for Moses. He chose him to lead his people out of Egypt's bondage and into the Promised Land. God chose a very poignant way of letting Moses in on his plan.

> **Now Moses was tending the flock of Jethro his father-in-law, the priest of Midian, and he led the flock to the far side of the desert and came to Horeb, the mountain of God. There the angel of the Lord appeared to him in flames of fire from within a bush. Moses saw that though the bush was on fire it did not burn up. So Moses thought, "I will go over and see this strange sight—why the bush does not burn up."**
>
> **When the Lord saw that he had gone over to look, God called to him from within the bush, "Moses! Moses!" And Moses said, "Here I am." Exodus 3:1-4**

Moses saw a burning bush. It appeared to be consumed with fire, yet it didn't burn up. Notice what Moses decided to go over, or turn aside, to see this strange sight. *After* Moses turned aside, God spoke to him.

Moses made a choice to turn aside from his busy work day and take the time to go check out this strange sight. My question is this: what would have happened if he had seen it but decided, "I'm too busy to go over there; it's probably just some campfire someone left burning."

God didn't call to Moses from the bush until Moses *chose* to turn aside and draw close.

Men, we have a choice to make. Every morning of our lives, from this day forward, we can choose to either rollover and hit the snooze button or turn aside to spend time with the God of the universe. What have we missed by not turning aside and seeking time in his presence?

Let's look at an analogy:

Pick something you enjoy doing and wish you did better—such as golf, tennis, hunting, fishing, working out—your choice. Let's run with golf for this illustration.

You play around at golf and just don't ever seem to get much better at it. You know you could be better if you played more, practiced more, or took a few lessons, but you just haven't devoted the time or money to it, so your game still pretty much stinks.

By chance, you enter a contest at the local golf course, and you get a phone call days later informing you that you have won. "Wow, I never win anything," you exclaim. "What did I win exactly?"

To your amazement, you discover that the grand prize is this: Phil Mickelson is coming by your house early Saturday morning to pick you up, fly you to his favorite country club, and spend the entire day playing golf with you. Even better, he is excited to do it and wants to hang out with you and help you with your game.

Unbelievable! One of the top golfers in the game is excited to spend the whole day playing golf with you and wants to help you work on my game. What an opportunity!

If you're like me, you would probably not get much sleep waiting for Saturday to arrive. On Saturday, you would most likely get out of bed extra early to get yourself ready, wipe down the old clubs, and be watching for his limo.
Okay – you're on to me by now.

Every single day of our lives, rain or shine, 365 days a year, the King of Kings, the Creator of the universe, our affectionate and wise heavenly Father "arrives" at our house to meet with us. He longs to spend the day with us and to help us with "our game."

All the wisdom, love, strength, peace, encouragement, and anything else we need is completely available to us, but the knob must be turned from our side of the door. (Read Revelation 3:20 again.) We must open the door to him. He will not push the door open and force his way in on our lives. He gave us a free will when he created us and the freedom to choose.

What would you miss if you hit the snooze and decide not to answer the door when Phil came to call? How would your golf game be different? How would it have made him feel?

What if after "the goddess" had expressed her love and affection for my son, he chose to never call or visit her again? What a loss that would have been for him. What we miss by not opening the door to Jesus tomorrow and every day thereafter is much more significant. We're not talking golf here. We are talking life—joy, peace, fulfillment, marriage, family, work, legacy; it's all here. Will we choose to turn our backs to God by leaving him outside knocking, or will we turn our faces to him by purposefully "turning aside" to walk with him?

If you find yourself in a position where you can honestly say, "God has never spoken to me," then you well might ask "Why should God speak to me? What am I doing in life that would make speaking to me a reasonable thing for Him to do? Are we in business together in life? Or am I in business just for myself, trying to 'use a little God' to advance my projects?"
~ Dallas Willard, Hearing God

How Do I Get There From Here? Part 2

Drawing Near

Moses did more than just notice the burning bush. He made a conscious choice. He chose to do something, to take action. He chose to *go over and see*. He chose to draw near.

> ***Draw near to God and He will draw near to you. James 4:8***

One of God's myriad promises to us is that if we will draw near to him, he will draw near to us.

He will engage us personally if we make the conscious effort to turn toward him. If we open the door, he promises to *come in and commune with us*. Much like the prodigal son's father ran to him when he saw him coming up the road, Jesus runs toward us if we turn and start in his direction. He longs to be near us, engage us, and shower us with his loving-kindness.

There's an important heart decision that needs to take place when turning aside. This decision will also profoundly affect your marriage. You must decide whether or not to become deliberate. Are you deliberate about your walk with Jesus? Are you deliberate about your approach to marriage and what God requires of you as a husband?

In order to excel in academics, sports, music, the arts, business, etc., it is a well-established fact that it takes practice and dogged determination. The great golfer Gary Player's legendary quote, "the harder I work, the luckier I get," is true in life, and it is especially true in marriage. Marriage only begins when you say "I do." It takes a lifetime to learn what you're doing. Relationships are fragile, and much is at stake.

It takes conscious daily effort and deliberateness to deny yourself, take up your cross daily, and follow Jesus, and it is by doing these things that we are strengthened, encouraged, and blown away by God's presence, wisdom, and power in our lives. Once we *taste and see that the Lord is good*, we will run to him and wake up excited to see what he says to us and how he leads us each day of our lives.

Men, we are not on a Christian cruise ship with our tickets to heaven punched. We can't wait out our arrival at heaven's gates by simply attending church, teaching a class or two along the way, reading some books, and remaining faithful to small group meetings. We need to get busy and stay on top of our game. We cannot remain neutral and simply hope that our personal lives and married lives will get better without effort. No one can do it for you. You are the only one who can decide to become more deliberate.

Listening to His Voice

When Moses turned aside and drew near – God spoke to him. God freely spoke to Adam, Noah, Abraham, David, Jesus, so why is it so hard to imagine that God would speak to you?

> *There is not in the world a kind of life more sweet and delightful than that of a continual conversation with God*
> Brother Lawrence, *The Practice of the Presence of God*

Listen to Jesus's words about recognizing his voice:

> **Let me set this before you as plainly as I can. If a person climbs over or through the fence of a sheep pen instead of going through the gate, you know he's up to no good—a sheep rustler! The shepherd walks right up to the gate. The gatekeeper opens the gate to him and the sheep recognize his voice. He calls his own sheep by name and leads them out. When he gets them all out, he leads them and they follow because they are familiar with his voice. They won't follow a stranger's voice but will scatter because they aren't used to the sound of it. John 10:1-5**

> *Jesus answered, "I told you, but you don't believe.*
> *Everything I have done has been authorized by my Father,*
> *actions that speak louder than words. You don't believe*
> *because you're not my sheep. My sheep recognize my*
> *voice. I know them, and they follow me. I give them real*
> *and eternal life. John 10:25-30*

Shepherds speak to their flock. The flock stays close enough to hear his voice and do what he says. He leads them to food, water, and shelter. He protects them and comforts them. They are under his 24/7 watchful eye.

God speaks to us. He wants to lead, bless, and protect us as well. He speaks through his word (the Bible), and his spirit speaks to our spirits. He loves us more than a shepherd loves his sheep. We are his children, and he wants to lead us, protect us, and provide for us. Real sheep instinctively know that the shepherd is there for their own good. They don't think twice about following. We, on the other hand, are born with the stubborn desire to listen to our own voices and follow our own ways. We instinctively feel that life is about us, and we need to busy ourselves getting everything done that is on our agendas for that day, week, month, and year.

> **But there is something we need to be honest about: part of us doesn't really want to hear what God has to say. I know something of this. I don't ask because I don't want to know. If I know what God thinks, then I'm faced with the decision of whether to follow his counsel or not. What was initially just a quandary or a moment of confusion becomes an issue of disobedience. I don't want that sort of clarity. Furthermore, I don't want God messing with my approach to life.**
> **~ John Eldredge, Walking with God**

Because of this, we have to train ourselves to listen to God. He speaks, but we are too busy or too noisy to hear. We rarely take time to simply be still and know that he is God. When is the last time you sat with God, TV off, radio off, cell phone off, and away from the office, family, hobbies, etc.? We rarely take the time to just commune with him, talking and listening.

I imagine God must feel like our wives do when they are trying to communicate with us, and we simply respond from behind the newspaper, "Uh huh. Yes, dear." Turning aside is important. Drawing near is critical.

But we have to quiet ourselves long enough to listen to what he is speaking, or else we are just going through the motions. We give ourselves brownie points for having a quick quiet time, reading a short devotional or scripture passage, and rushing off to do what we have on our agendas. We read the Bible, but we miss the God of the Bible. We are religious, but we lack true relationship. There is a huge difference!

Doing What He Says

My older brother and I would play outside almost every afternoon after school. Our football games or war games only ended because we heard mom shouting out the window, "Boys, come in. It's time for supper!"

More often than not, we simply played on. "Time for supper, boys!" she hailed again. We played on. "Dinner's on the table. Come in *now*!" We finally ran for the door.

We heard Mom's words. We heard her voice. We even picked up on her volume, her higher pitch, and her sense of urgency, but we still played on. It was only when we felt in danger that we obeyed. Sound familiar? We all do it. None of us naturally wants to obey the rules, especially when they inconvenience us or get in our way. Remember, we are born into it. We think, *Life is about me and what I want. (Surely everyone knows this and should cut me some slack.)*

As we all know, rules are generally created for our own good. Don't touch the hot stove. Don't run out into the street. Wear your coat outside in the winter. Wash your hands. On and on they go. We didn't like them as kids, and we don't like them any more when we are grown. There is something in us that resists obeying.

Men, in particular, are hard-headed. We seem to have a more obstinate and rebellious nature than women do. This is why men, in general, find it much harder to humble ourselves and follow someone. That is why it irritates us to read scriptures that speak of submitting to one another, denying ourselves, and following Jesus. Besides, most of the pictures I have ever seen of Jesus don't portray him as someone I would want to follow anyway. Maybe he would grant me an exemption.

Jesus said very plainly when asked what one must do to be a Christian (Christ-follower), "Deny yourself, take up your cross daily, and follow me." (Mark 8:34) It doesn't get much simpler than that. But, if I am honest, I really don't want to deny myself (anything), and I sure don't like the idea of dying to my agenda and goals for my life (I think I can do just fine, thank you). And then I have to follow him? Dang it! This is asking too much. What if he wants to lead me somewhere I really don't want to go, or what if it conflicts with my plans for my life?

You want the bottom line? Well, the bottom line is this: at any moment in our day, we are either following Jesus, or we are leading our own lives. We are the shepherds of our lives, or we are his sheep. There really is no middle ground.

If you really want to know what it takes to truly walk with God and experience the life and marriage he intended, here's the truth:

1. Realize that this kind of life (walking with our God) is not only possible, but it is what we are created for.
2. Begin to make deliberate choices to pursue him no matter what.
3. Discipline yourself to take the time to draw near to him.
4. Still yourself enough to be able to hear his voice throughout the day.
5. Even if you don't completely understand it, obey what he tells you.
6. Trust him to lead you in every facet of your life. (He loves you unconditionally and has only your best in mind; he is sovereign and faithful.)
7. Fellowship with other men who are also deliberate about following him.

Welcome to the Front Lines

As if the seven previous exhortations above aren't hard enough – there is one more thing you must be aware of. You have an enemy—a diabolically dangerous enemy who hates the fact that you want to turn your face toward God and begin living your life in close relationship with him. He (Satan) hated Adam and Eve, and he has hated everyone in God's family ever since. We are at war. And war is hell.

I can assure you that if you truly desire, and commit, to live your life following the truths we have just discussed, you will encounter strong resistance. Don't let it deter or discourage you. Just know it will come, and be ready. Proverbs 4:23 tells us to *guard our heart*.

Many books have been written concerning our nemesis, and I recommend reading some of them. For our purposes, let me simply alert you again to the fact that our enemy is committed to trying to destroy you, your wife and kids, your marriage, your financial life, and your witness and ministry. He is not a cartoon character in a devil costume. He will try any scheme, any deception, any lie, and any plan to ruin your emotional, physical, and spiritual life. Because you are a Christian, he knows he cannot "unsave" you, but he can make your life here on earth hell if you let him.

Let me point out a couple of things Jesus said about Satan:

> The thief [Satan] comes only to steal and kill and destroy; I have come that they may have life, and have it abundantly. *John 10:10*

> But the Son of God came to destroy the works of the devil. *1 John 3:8b*

Jesus, our perfect shepherd, came to earth to destroy the work of Satan. He totally obliterated the work and effect of Adam and Eve's sin by spilling his blood on our behalf and paying the price for sin. All mankind now has a way to once again have eternal life in God's presence as we live here on earth and after we die.

Satan, however, is still called:

"our adversary/enemy"
1 Peter 5:8
Matthew 13:38b

"the evil/wicked one"
Matthew 13:19
Matthew 13:38b

"The serpent"
Genesis 3:1-15
2 Corinthians 11:3

"The tempter"
Matthew 4:3
1 Thessalonians 3:5

"The father of lies"
John 8:44

"The accuser of the brethren"
Revelation 12:10b

"The prince/ruler of this world"
John 12:31
John 14:30

"The god of this world"
2 Corinthians 4:4

He and his minions still roam the planet "seeking whom he may devour." (1 Peter 5:8) Jesus reminds us in scripture that we live in a world at war. Most Christians, me included, have read something about that in the Bible, but we go about our daily lives oblivious to the war raging around us.

We experience it every day. Those pesky thoughts that haunt us about the buxom secretary, the magnetic pull toward porn sites on our computers, the voice that whispers it is okay to waste time at work playing solitaire, and the thousands of other thoughts that flood our souls every day. Do we just come up with these on our own? Not at all—we live in a world at war.

Analogy #2

You go to sleep tonight and drift off into a beautiful REM sleep filled with pleasant thoughts. Ahhh … a great night's sleep for a change. Perfect. Then you are jolted out of your sleep in the early morning by a sound like thunder, but it seems so close. Did lightening hit my house, you wonder? Not exactly. You wake up on the front lines of the war in Iraq. Somehow you have been transported to Iraq and are waking up in a tent with dozens of other scurrying GIs. They are all throwing on their fatigues, flak jackets, and helmets; grabbing their assault rifles; and hurrying outside. You look around and see that all you have on are your jogging shorts, a white T-shirt, and tennis shoes. The war is on your doorstep, and you're not ready to fight. And let me tell you, the enemy won't wait for you to suit up.

Silly as it may seem, the vast majority of Christians wake up every single day and walk through a blazing, dangerous war zone with no clue. They see evidence of war all around them and may even be deeply wounded or affected personally, but they are somehow content to just press on—on their way to getting stuff done, checking things off their daily to-do list.

The Holy Spirit, writing through Paul, implores us in Ephesians 6:13–18:

> Therefore put on the full armor of God, so that when the day of evil comes, you may be able to stand your ground, and after you have done everything, to stand. Stand firm then, with the belt of truth buckled around your waist, with the breastplate of righteousness in place, and with your feet fitted with the readiness that comes from the gospel of peace. In addition to all this, take up the shield of faith, with which you can extinguish all the flaming arrows of the evil one. Take the helmet of salvation and the sword of the Spirit, which is the word of God. And pray in the Spirit on all occasions with all kinds of prayers and requests. With this in mind, be alert and always keep on praying for all the saints.

Whether we believe it or not, whether we accept it or not, we live in a war zone. We have an enemy who is hell-bent on our destruction. He doesn't play favorites, and he doesn't care. He will relentlessly tempt you. He will continually try to drive a wedge between you and your wife and children. He will haunt your children with nightmares and rebellious thoughts. He seeks to inflame strife, anger, and resentment between you and your wife. If God's design in marriage is to make you and your spouse one, then it is Satan's macabre mission to separate you into two.

> *Finally, let the Lord make you strong. Depend on his mighty power. Put on all of God's armor. Then you can stand firm against the devil's evil plans. Our fight is not against human beings. It is against the rulers, the authorities and the powers of this dark world. It is against the spiritual forces of evil in the heavenly world. (Ephesians 6:10-12)*

Men, we have no choice. We must learn to defend ourselves and our families. Otherwise, we are sitting ducks. Knowing God's truth, walking close to him, hearing his voice, and obeying him in this area is critical. Don't be deceived into thinking this isn't real. Jesus, his disciples, and the early church all faced this enemy. Why should we be exempt?

Thankfully, Jesus has given us all the authority and tools we need to overcome this enemy. It is our responsibility to use these tools every day if we are to experience that victory in our lives and in our marriages.

Truth - Jesus has already won the war and has all authority over the enemy.

Colossians 2:15 "And having *disarmed* the powers and authorities, he made a public spectacle of them, *triumphing over them* by the cross."

Ephesians 1:18-23 "I pray also that the eyes of your heart may be enlightened in order that you may know the hope to which he has called you, the riches of his glorious inheritance in the saints, and his incomparably great power for us who believe. That power is like the working of his mighty strength, which he exerted in Christ when *he raised him from the dead and seated him at his right hand in the heavenly realms, far above all rule and authority, power and dominion, and every title that can be given, not only in the present age but also in the one to come. And God placed all things under his feet* and appointed him to be head over everything for the church, which is his body, the fullness of him who fills everything in every way."

Truth - He gave authority to the disciples.

Matthew 10:1 "He called his twelve disciples to him and *gave them authority* to drive out evil spirits and to heal every disease and sickness."

Truth - He gave authority to others

Luke 10:17–20 "The seventy-two returned with joy and said, 'Lord, even the demons submit to us in your name.' He replied, 'I saw Satan fall like lightning from heaven. *I have given you authority* to trample on snakes and scorpions and *to overcome all the power of the enemy*; nothing will harm you. However, do not rejoice that the spirits submit to you, but rejoice that your names are written in heaven.'"

Truth - He gives the same authority to us.

Ephesians 2:4–6 "But because of his great love for us, God, who is rich in mercy, made us alive with Christ even when we were dead in transgressions— it is by grace you have been saved. And God raised us up with Christ and seated us with him in the heavenly realms in Christ Jesus."

2 Corinthians 10:3–5 "For though we live in the world, *we* do not *wage war* as the world does. The weapons *we fight with* are not the weapons of the world. On the contrary, they have *divine power to demolish strongholds. We demolish* arguments and every pretension that sets itself up against the knowledge of God, and *we take captive* every thought to make it obedient to Christ."

James 4:7 "Submit yourselves, then, to God. Resist the devil, and he will flee from you."

We wake every morning to a world at war—whether we believe it or not, whether we agree with it or not, whether we prepare for it or not.

The more we know about it and how to fight it, the better off our marriages and families will be. Even though we are on the winning side, we all know people whose lives, marriages, and children have been decimated by the sinister work of Satan. Satan's biggest weapon is his mouth. He is a liar, accuser, and deceiver. His biggest deception of all is that he really doesn't exist, and there really isn't a war. Then we spend all our energy warring against our spouses and children—and even God—instead of the real foe.

> *For we wrestle not against flesh and blood, but against principalities, against powers, against the rulers of the darkness of this world, against spiritual wickedness in high places. Ephesians 6:12*

If you are really serious about walking in an intimate, daily relationship with God, I can assure you that such a decision will not sit well with the powers of darkness. They will ramp up their efforts to distract, discourage, and defeat you.

So, be alert, be on your guard, and fight. Resist the devil, and he **will** flee from you. That verse is a promise from God's very mouth. It doesn't say he might flee. Our responsibility is to resist and believe God's word.

Where Does This Battle Take Place?

Look again at 2 Corinthians 10:3–5. Notice that we war against arguments, pretensions, and thoughts. It is obvious that the battlefield is in our minds. If Satan can get us to believe and act on his lies, deceptions, and accusations, he can gain strongholds in our minds and, thus, our lives. Remember God's word: "As a man thinketh, so is he" (Proverbs 23:7).

We must decide nearly every minute of every day whether we will listen to and believe the lies of the enemy or accept and trust in the truth of our God. That is why it is so critical that we know what God's word says. If not, we begin to reason with Satan and mull over his deceptions in our minds (like Eve did), and we will lose. We need to refute lies with the truth (like Jesus did).

I am so thankful that we don't have to live our lives in fear of (or under the power of) this enemy. Even though he is quite powerful and diabolically deceiving and clever, Jesus has triumphed over him. Not only that, but he has disarmed him. Take a minute to read Colossians 2:15. Jesus took Satan's weapons away.
We are not as powerful as Satan, but we have authority over him in Jesus. At the name of Jesus, demons tremble, obey, and flee. Each of us has all the authority and weaponry we need to win the daily skirmishes we face. We, however, have to use them. God will not do it for us.

Much like salvation, we must accept God's provision by faith (our freedom and authority in his name) and walk in it.

Also remember, Satan cannot read our thoughts. Like Jesus, we must resist him verbally – out loud. We can't merely think to ourselves "satan leave me alone right now". We have to speak the words. We need to speak the word of God (as did Jesus) and command Satan to leave our thoughts, our bodies, our homes, etc. Don't allow him to torment you, or those you love, any longer.

> *You, dear children, are from God and have overcome them, because the one who is in you is greater than the one who is in the world. 1 John 4:4*

I Thought We Were Talking about Marriage

You are correct. The sole purpose in writing this book is to talk straight to men about their marriage relationships. Furthermore, the intent is to cut to the chase and get to the bottom line. What are the real keys to a successful, fulfilling marriage?

Men want the bottom line. They want to skip to the end of the story and see what happens. *Spare me all the details. What do I need to know?*

Men also want things convenient and easy. *Don't disrupt my happy life, just give me a couple of bullet points and let's get this done.* Sadly, most men are downright lazy, if we are honest. We gravitate to those things that come fairly easily for us and that we don't have to work very hard for. We all want to play in the game but would rather not have to practice.

God created marriage and has established the playbook for a successful one. Sure, there's lots of great advice out there, like the top ten tools to effective communication and understanding why men are like waffles and why women are like spaghetti. However, if we are ever to experience marriage in its highest form, we will have to practice and play by his rules.

The Bottom Line
(The Reason You're Reading This Book)

1. Turn your life and marriage over to God. This is a daily process, not a one-time choice.
2. Focus on what God is saying to you regarding your marriage, and trust him speak to your wife about her issues.
3. Draw near to Him each and every day, from today on, and ask Him to work in your heart to both will and to do of His good pleasure. Listen for His voice and do what He tells you- whether you understand it or feel like it.
4. Remember it is primarily your responsibility to set the spiritual and emotional tone in your home. Be the first to seek God. Be first at having a humble, servant heart and an attitude of thankfulness. Be first to say you are sorry when you screw up, and ask her forgiveness.
5. Learn what the Bible says about marriage and your responsibilities in it. Then ask him to help you *do* it.
6. Be prepared for a fight and resist the lies that will be hurled at you daily from the enemy. Deal with personal strongholds/habits/agreements in your life.
7. Find a mentor, close friend, or group of guys who will walk with you on this journey.

8. Acknowledge that there are no Cliff's Notes—no easy way out. Be deliberate about obeying God's word and being the man you need to be as a husband, regardless of her actions or responses.

9. Don't rely on emotions. Obey God. Don't give up. You will be tempted to throw in the towel.

10. Know that his reward is far beyond what you can hope for right now. Trust him. His plans for you are "good."

It is no use working on the symptoms of a less-than-desirable marriage. Spend whatever time it takes working on the cause. The real cause is not your wife, your past sins and issues, or even your circumstances.

We don't have a wife problem—we have a Jesus problem. We are simply not walking with him. We want a fulfilling, Christian marriage and a happy home life, but we are not walking in relationship with the God who created marriage.

Whenever my old football team would lose a game, our coach would always bark at us in the locker room, "Blocking and tackling. That's what we need to work on—the basics. We need to get back to the basics, blocking and tackling."

Legendary Green Bay Packers coach Vince Lombardi was famous for his memorable creed, "You block and tackle better than the team you're playing, you win." It is true in football and truer still in marriage. God instructs men and women how to "block and tackle" in marriage. His word is very specific and powerful and explains the basics, the foundational blocks of a healthy and enjoyable marriage. We not only need to hear it and know it, but we also need to *do* it.

When asked his secret of love, being married fifty-four years to the same person, Billy Graham said, "Ruth and I are happily incompatible."

In Closing...

Men are notorious loners. If we're honest, we are also typically very insecure. We avoid becoming vulnerable with others for fear of being thought of as weak or a failure. Our pride keeps us from saying, "I blew it, I'm sorry," "I need help," or "I don't know how."

It's just the way we're wired. Somewhere back in our grade school life, we were made fun of, were laughed at, or felt vastly inferior to the "other guys." Man, I sure did.

I recently saw a picture of my wife and me when we were in the ninth grade. Yes, I married my high school sweetheart. At the time, she was taller than me, and she is only five feet, three inches tall. I was a late bloomer and didn't begin to grow taller and bigger until late in the ninth grade. Junior high, as you might imagine, was brutal.

I came from an elementary school where I was king of the playground. I could run faster, jump higher, and play kickball better than anyone in school. The girls liked me; the boys liked me. Heck, even the principal liked me. I was on top of the world and then came junior high. Overnight I became a wimp, a wuss, a dweeb—a nobody.

I know that it was during this time in my life that I began to withdraw emotionally and hide my inadequacies. I am sure I told thousands of lies and half-truths simply to cover my frail emotions.

The point is that we all have insecurities and fears. We all feel inferior in some way and hide from people. We try and mask over our secret hurts with success in business or hobbies. We are desperate to find something we are competent at. We long to be praised, respected, and looked up to. We want to be somebody.

Marriage is no different. None of us has it down. We all fake it. When asked how things are going at home, we most often answer, "Fine." We dare not share with a friend or a group that we are struggling in some area of our marriages for fear of being thought a failure or, worse yet, a poor leader. So we stuff it. We stay in hiding. Or we blow up like a peacock to hide our insecurity. We get angry. We yell and bully our wives in order to get our way.

God wants to tell you to come out of hiding. He knows all about your feelings, your hurts, your fears, your failures, and your past. He loves you more than anyone ever has or ever will. Only he can reach deep inside your soul and restore you. Turn the doorknob and let him come in and live life with you. You will be amazed by his affection and captivated by his wisdom. You've tried marriage on your terms. Why not try it his way?

Remember, we are all born into this world of sin and automatically have a life-stunting addiction—ourselves. We are self-centered and self-focused from birth, much like a computer has default settings for certain applications that have to be manually overwritten if you want to change them. The default setting on our hard drives is "me." As Christians, we must make a daily (if not hourly) decision to manually, deliberately overwrite that setting.

Another way to look at it is similar to walking the wrong way up an escalator or paddling against the current on a float trip. If you stop walking or stop paddling, you automatically revert back to the direction of the primary force. There is no neutral. At any moment in our day we are either moving toward Jesus or moving away from him. We either have our face toward him or our back toward him. As you know, paddling against the current of a river is hard work. It takes effort. It is easier just to go with the flow – but the "flow" may get us to a waterfall downstream.

Each of us has choices to make from the moment our eyes open each morning until we shut them at night. More books, seminars, and sermons will not do the trick, although they are incredibly valuable, and we should run to them for knowledge and insight.

No, what you and I need is not more information but transformation. We need a completely new paradigm for living life and living marriage. Only a daily, personal relationship with the Author of life and marriage will provide us with the power, wisdom, and joy to fully enjoy them both as they were created to be enjoyed.

I cannot describe it, I seldom refer to it, it is almost too sacred an experience to name....I can only say God revealed Himself to me, and I had such an experience of His love that I had to ask Him to stay His hand. I would not now be placed back where I was before that blessed experience if you should give me all the world; it would be as small dust in the balance.

~ Dwight L. Moody

Another suggestion:

Do whatever it takes to find a close friend or an older mentor to walk with on this journey. You have the best of intentions (just like I do when I want to lose weight and get back in shape), but will most likely slow to a crawl or stop after a short while without a mentor or friend to encourage you. Remember, none of us has arrived. We're all on a journey. The goal is progress, not perfection.

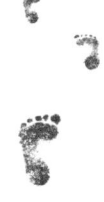

Also, let us hear from you as you begin your journey walking with God in your marriage. If you can't find a mentor in your local area or need additional help on your journey, please contact us. We are developing additional materials, Web sites, and mentor partners across the country to better help men enjoy the amazing adventure of walking with God and experiencing his blessing and abundance in their marriages.

Email Square1 Ministries: marriagesthatmatter@gmail.com

Visit our Web site: www.square1ministries.com

Visit our blog, which is especially designed for and about husbands: huzband.wordpress.com

Order more books for friends or small group study by ordering from our website, or email us for quantity discounts.

"For I know the plans I have for you," declares the Lord, "plans to prosper you and not to harm you, plans to give you hope and a future."
~ Jeremiah 29:11

May God bless you beyond your wildest dreams.
May He receive glory from your life and from your marriage.

The 30-Day Challenge

"I bet I can belch louder than you."
"I dare you to ask that girl out."
"Wanna bet some money on that?"

Men love a challenge. It seems there is something in us that springs to life when we have "skin in the game."

Challenge or not, you have plenty of skin in your marriage! You have everything to gain and everything to lose. While it is definitely not a game, it is the most important challenge of your life.

That is precisely why I decided to add a challenge for you. Maybe a challenge will bring to life that part of you that needs a dare, a bet, a goal, and a quest to pursue. Men risk their lives for things that seem important to them—that meet a deep need in their souls to achieve, finish, or conquer a challenge.

Men have died climbing mountains, racing automobiles, snow skiing down dangerous peaks, and sailing around the world. Why? To see if they could do something no man has ever done before or to do something better than it has ever been done.

I would like to challenge you to do something for thirty days, and it may cost you your life. Not your physical life, but your self-seeking life that encourages you to be lazy in your relationship with Jesus and with your wife. There is the possibility here for enormous breakthrough, amazing adventure, and life transformation, but it does cost you something.

The two currencies I ask you to spend on this challenge are these: your time and your pride. Both carry tremendous value to us as men. Our vocabulary is filled with personal pronouns. We use phrases such as my time, my plans, my money, and my rights. Our lives are filled with "I deserve its." We have come to expect, and even feel like we deserve, things like tranquility, comfort, success, happiness, respect, health and fun.

It is not that God, in his love, does not want us to experience these things, but he does not want us to turn these goals into gods or idols above him. He is the one to be pursued, not these pleasurable, worldly and temporary things (see Matthew 6:33).

The purpose of the challenge is not to "fix" everything in thirty days. It is not to spend thirty days doing something hard in order to live the rest of your days pursuing self-gratification.

The purpose is to help you gain traction on a lifestyle, a journey, that you were created by God to experience and to give you an on-ramp to a different paradigm of living as a Christ-follower.

This challenge will begin to transform your marriage and your personal life. These thirty days are only a beginning. What happens after they are over is up to no one but you. Your life, and your marriage, will only be as fulfilling as your daily walk with Christ.

The Challenge primarily focuses on two things:

1. Devoting yourself more fully to God
2. Devoting yourself more fully to your wife

The first step must be #1. You cannot do the second step until you are doing the first step.

If you are ready to press ahead and accept the Challenge, here's what you do first:

Email me at *marriagesthatmatter@gmail.com* and order the 30-Day Challenge material. Along with your devotional you will also have our commitment to pray for you personally during the following thirty days.

If you need any encouragement or have any questions along the way, don't hesitate to email us also. We are here to help, to cheer, and to pray that God will honor your decision to move closer to him and to your wife and bless you beyond measure.

Remember that you will face stiff competition during this Challenge. We will be fighting with you and believing God for breakthroughs in your walk with him and with your wife.

> *I am asking God, the glorious Father of our Lord Jesus Christ, to give you spiritual wisdom and insight so that you might grow in your knowledge of Him. I pray that your hearts will be flooded with light so that you can understand the confident hope he has given to those he called—his holy people who are his rich and glorious inheritance. I also pray that you will understand the incredible greatness of God's power for us who believe him.*
>
> *~ Ephesians 1:17-19*

"husband" A USERS GUIDE
Leaders Guide

Prior to meeting #1

- Meet with your man/men to give them a general overview of the material and cast a vision for the results anticipated from studying this material together, ie:
    - A happier, healthier marriage
    - A closer, more rewarding walk with Christ
    - A spiritual and marital legacy to pass down to your children & grandchildren

- Assume the man/men you are meeting with desire to learn more about marriage, but don't assume they are saved or are walking with Christ every day. Don't even assume they know how to do that.

- Tell him/them you expect them to read the assigned material and to make note of what scriptures, notes or quotes speak to their heart. Set the expectation that they are expected to "do something" (not just attend class) and come prepared to interact and share what they feel they are hearing from God.

- Tell them there will be a few "projects" during the class that will call for courage to engage their wife. They should be willing to get her involved and learn from her input.

- Remind them that even though God promises to help them become a great husband (if they follow Him), He will hold them personally accountable for the health of their marriage.
    - Hand out the initial wife assessment* to be taken home and completed by their wife. It is to be sealed inside an envelope and delivered, unopened to you at the first meeting. *this tool is to provide a baseline for assessing whether the class actually helps a husband make progress. There will be a follow up assessment at the end of class.*
        - This tool will not be opened or shared with the husband or the class
        - Class results will be sent to Square1Ministries in order to measure the effectiveness of these resources.

- Remind them that they have a formidable enemy who does not want them to make progress in their marriage. They should expect an increase in spiritual warfare at home, and resistance to their effort to complete their assignments and even to attending class on a regular basis.

Hand out the husband book and make meeting 1 assignment – pages 7-18

The book is divided into four parts, with "chapters" within those parts.

Part one
Laying the foundation that marriage is God's idea, and that He is a loving father who only has "good plans" in His heart for His children – and their marriages.

- Meeting #1 – review pages 7-18
- Meeting #2 – review pages 19-27

Part two
This foundational section lays the groundwork for Christian marriage as desired, and commanded, by the Author of marriage. This part will take at least two meetings to fully explore. Don't hurry through this part. Stop wherever your time allows. Take as much time as you feel necessary to adequate get the message of God's Word across.

- Meeting #3 – review pages 28-35
- Meeting #4 – review pages 35-47

Part three
Additional biblical truths regarding relationships and how God expects us to treat each other. This is also the introduction to communication in marriage and the power of our words.

- Meeting #5 – review pages 48-54
- Meeting #6 – review pages 55-65

Part four
Overview of the practical, how-do-I-do-this issues of being a husband, and walking with God. Last session is a crucial lesson on spiritual warfare. Husbands have got to learn this lesson in order to lead and protect their wife and family. *encourage your man/men to take the 30-Day Challenge if they want to make significant progress in their marriage and their walk with Christ.

- Meeting #7 – review pages 66-78
- Meeting #8 – review pages 79-89 (90-91)*

2 Timothy 2:2
The things which you have heard from me in the presence of many witnesses, entrust these to faithful men who will be able to teach others also.

NOTES

NOTES

www.ingramcontent.com/pod-product-compliance
Lightning Source LLC
Chambersburg PA
CBHW071725040426
42446CB00011B/2214